THE MEANING OF SANCTIFICATION

MY TESTIMONY

By E. Stanley Jones

I came to Christ bankrupt. My capacity to blunder drove me to his feet, and to my astonishment he took me, forgave me, and sent my happy soul singing its way down the years. By grace was I saved, through faith, and that not of myself—it was the gift of God.

I walked in the joy of that for months and then the clouds began to gather. There was something within me not redeemed, something else down in the cellar that seemed to be sullenly at war with this new life, I was at war with myself.

I think I can see what happened. We live in two minds—the conscious and the subconscious. The subconscious is the residing place of the driving instincts: self, sex, and the herd. These instincts have come down through a long racial history and they have bents toward evil.

Into the conscious mind there is introduced at conversion a new life, a new Loyalty, a new love. But the subconscious mind does not obey this new life. Its driving instincts drive for fulfillment apart from any morality built up in the conscious mind. There ensues a clash between the new life in the conscious mind and the instincts of the subconscious. The house of man-soul becomes a house divided against itself.

I wondered if this was the best that Christianity could do—to leave one in this divided condition? I found to my glad surprise the teaching concerning the Holy Spirit, and I found that the area of the work of the Holy Spirit is largely, if not entirely, in the subconscious. I found that if I would surrender to the Holy Spirit this conscious mind—all I knew and all I did not know—He would cleanse at these depths I could not control. I surrendered and accepted the gift by faith. He did cleanse as a refining fire. In that cleansing there was a unifying. Conscious and subconscious minds were brought under a single control and redemption. That control was the Holy Spirit. I was no longer at war with myself. Life was on a permanently higher level. It was no longer up and down. The soul had caught its stride. I went on my way singing a new song. That song has continued. It is fresher today than then.

Editor's Note: *Dr. Jones's testimony was written for this book at the request of the author.*

THE MEANING OF SANCTIFICATION

By Charles Ewing Brown, D.D.

Francis Asbury Press
Distributed by Warner Press
Anderson, Indiana

Coordinator of Publishing & Creative Services
Church of God Ministries, Inc.
PO Box 2420
Anderson, IN 46018-2420
800-848-2464
www.chog.org

To purchase additional copies of this book, to inquire about distribution, and for all other sales-related matters, please contact:

Warner Press, Inc.
PO Box 2499
Anderson, IN 46018-2499
800-741-7721
www.warnerpress.org

ISBN-13: 978-1-59317-627-3

Printed in the United States of America.
14 15 16 17 18 / TPS / 10 9 8 7 6 5 4 3 2

Miserable thou art, wheresoever thou be, or whithersoever thou turnest, unless thou turn thyself unto God.

Why art thou troubled when things succeed not as thou wouldest or desirest? For who is he that hath all things according to his mind? neither I nor thou, nor any man upon earth.

There is none in this world, even though he be king or bishop, without some tribulation or perplexity. Who is then in the best case [or condition]? even he who is able to suffer something for God.

Thomas à Kempis, in THE IMITATION OF CHRIST (Fifteenth Century)

For as you excel all men in intelligence, you know that those whose life is directed towards God as its rule, so that each one among us may be blameless and irreproachable before Him, will not entertain even the thought of the slightest sin. For if we believed that we should live only the present life, then we might be suspected of sinning, through being enslaved to flesh and blood, or overmastered by gain or carnal desire.

Athenagoras, in A PLEA FOR THE CHRISTIANS (Second Century)

As for those who are persuaded that nothing will escape the scrutiny of God, but that even the body which has ministered to the irrational impulses of the soul, and to its desires, will be punished along with it, it is not likely that they will commit even the smallest sin.

Athenagoras, in A PLEA FOR THE CHRISTIANS (Second Century)

And when the people transgressed the law which had been given to them by God, God being good and pitiful, unwilling to destroy them, in addition to His giving them the law, afterwards sent forth also prophets to them from among their brethren, to teach and remind them of the contents of the law, and to turn them to repentance, that they might sin no more.

Theophilus to Autolycus (Second Century)

Still, alas! the old Man doth live in me, he is not wholly crucified, is not perfectly dead.

Still doth he mightily strive against the Spirit, and stirreth up inward wars, and suffereth not the kingdom of my soul to be in peace.

For the love of God thou oughtest cheerfully to undergo all things, that is to say, all labor, grief, temptation, vexation, anxiety, necessity, infirmity, injury, detraction, reproof, humiliation, shame, correction, and contempt [of every kind and degree].

Thomas à Kempis, in THE IMITATION OF CHRIST (Fifteenth Century)

There is need of thy grace [O Lord], and of great degrees thereof, that nature may be overcome, which is ever prone to evil from her youth.

For through Adam the first man, nature being fallen and corrupted by sin the penalty of this stain hath descended upon all mankind, in such sort, that "nature" itself, which by thee was created good and upright, is now taken for the sin and infirmity of corrupted nature; because the inclination thereof left unto itself draweth to evil and to inferior things.

Thomas à Kempis, in THE IMITATION OF CHRIST (Fifteenth Century)

Ah! fool, why dost thou think to live long, when thou canst not promise to thyself one day?

How many have been deceived and suddenly snatched away!

How often dost thou hear these reports: Such a man is slain, another man is drowned, a third breaks his neck with a fall from some high place, this man died eating, and that man playing!

One perished by fire, another by the sword, another of the plague, another was slain by thieves. Thus death is the end of all, and man's life suddenly passeth away like a shadow.

Thomas à Kempis, in THE IMITATION OF CHRIST (Fifteenth Century)

To the congregation
Who listened to my first Sermon
on or about
September 3, 1895
and to
All those to whom I have
since ministered
the Word of God,
In solemn remembrance.

CONTENTS

FOREWORD

Charles E. Brown (1883–1971) was born in Illinois and by age eleven was traveling with his father Willis as a holiness evangelist in Illinois, Missouri, and Kentucky. In 1902 they contacted and affiliated with the young Church of God movement (Anderson, Indiana). Charles attended Asbury College and joined the Methodist Church, but he soon re-affiliated with the Church of God and was ordained in 1903.[1] He resumed evangelistic work and would pastor congregations in New York, Pennsylvania, Michigan, and Indiana. Although he was a longtime member of the Missionary Board of the Church of God, beginning in 1921, and held other national ministry posts, his major ministry would be in Christian writing and publishing.

AN EDITOR-WRITER WITH BALANCE

In 1930 Brown was elected the fourth editor of the *Gospel Trumpet*, the holiness periodical launched in 1880 by Daniel S. Warner, primary pioneer of the Church of God movement. Brown immediately announced his intention that this prominent periodical would be an "instrument in the hands of God for the promotion of deep spirituality and of the Great Revival of Holy Ghost religion for which humanity today languishes."[2] The prolific writing ministry of Charles Brown chronicled the developing life of the Church of God

1. Much interesting detail is found in Lee Dean Preston, "Charles E. Brown: His Life and Influence. . .," master's thesis, Iliff School of Theology, Denver, CO, 1969.

2. Charles E. Brown, in the *Gospel Trumpet*, July 3, 1930, 25.

movement across its first generations.[3] Not satisfied to merely recount history, he also worked hard at grounding the self-perception and teaching tradition of the Church of God movement in a more informed historical understanding than had been the case. While not a formally trained historian, Brown read widely and developed a strong sense of the importance of history for understanding the present.

Determined not to be just another "dumb preacher" in a time when many were suspicious of formal education, Brown studied Greek, Latin, Hebrew, and German, making him a "liberal" in some eyes. He certainly was willing to think newly, one definition of a liberal. He encouraged the Church of God movement to reconsider itself within the fuller spectrum of the history of the broader church. He came to see the movement as "an experiment in spiritual democracy," one that "makes a solid and valuable contribution to the story of the church's age-long struggle with the world and of its march toward that unity which all its members covet."[4]

Brown was loyal to the Church of God movement, but he was not a blind follower of its pioneer thinkers. He emerged over the years as a vital link between the thought of the early movement and what he judged to be more responsible historically and more workable for the coming future. By the 1940s, the movement had grown substantially and developed considerable organization within its life. This development was permitted because of practical necessity and had created

3. Charles E. Brown, *When the Trumpet Sounded: A History of the Church of God Reformation Movement* (Anderson, Indiana: Warner Press, 1951).

4. Ibid., xi-xii.

significant tension with the vigorous anti-organization stance of the earlier movement thinkers, who were staunch "come-outers" from all church organizations. Brown helped to relieve this tension by making a careful distinction. Believers are free and even responsible to introduce necessary organization in the *work* of the church—after all, that was done in the early church; believers, however, are not free to attempt to organize *the church itself*.[5]

The pioneers of the Church of God had spoken of the "Last Reformation," thinking that the church would be restored to its apostolic purity before the imminent return of the Lord. However, Brown's generation was beginning to realize that this imminent-return assumption had been premature and could even be irresponsible. His own research led him to the conclusion that reading the Bible through largely apocalyptic eyes risks a misreading of the past in favor of an immediate and shortsighted reforming enthusiasm.

The Church of God movement, Brown realized, was not a completely new and necessarily final aspect of God's plan. In fact, holiness reformation was an ancient theme in church history. The life-giving water of inspired reform had flowed for centuries, creating ancient valleys now being traveled by this movement. Brown saw and honored both these valleys and the movement he had come to see backlit with their ancient wisdom.

5. Charles E. Brown, "The Visible and Invisible Church," *Gospel Trumpet*, February 9, 1946, 2.

SANCTIFICATION IS BIBLICAL AND APOSTOLIC

The classic 1947 Brown book titled *The Apostolic Church* searches for the standard by which all of church history may be judged fairly and all present reforming efforts informed and inspired. He determined that the teachings of the apostolic era, as set forth in the New Testament, are the standard of Christian doctrine for all time. For Brown, a key element of this foundational apostolic teaching is the subject of sanctification. He insists that "the church of the first century firmly believed and clearly taught, not only the possibility, but the stern necessity of *living above sin*."[6] Such mature Christian faith, in Brown's view, is the only key that will open the possibility of true Christian unity and effective world evangelization. This conviction, while lost in much of the church's history, had been on a long journey of return.

Brown connected the Church of God movement with what he called the "Great Revival." Following the sixteenth-century Protestant Reformation, the first phase of this apostolic recovery was the seventeenth-century movement commonly known as Pietism, which emphasized *regeneration*. The second phase was the call to *sanctification* or holiness associated with the eighteenth-century reforming ministries of Charles and John Wesley. The first phase resisted a dead formality in church life and the second urged believers to go "on to perfection." These led to the third revival stage involving the Spirit-inspired impulse for the church, in her recovered holiness, to overcome her own tragic dividedness.

6. Brown, *The Apostolic Church*, 67. Emphasis added.

In effect, the three stages of the church's journey back to the fullness of Pentecost's biblical faith and Spirit-filled life are answers to the prayers of Jesus for his disciples of all time:

1. "Father, forgive them" (Luke 23:34);
2. "Sanctify them through thy truth" (John 17:17); and
3. "That they all may be one" (John 17:21).

In Brown's view, this trilogy forms the heart of the Christian gospel itself, and also what the Church of God movement is trying to accomplish on behalf of the contemporary church.

These reforming stages led through Martin Luther and the Anabaptists to John Wesley and his followers and ultimately to the unity emphasis of John Winebrenner (b. 1797) that led to the reforming work of Daniel Warner (1842-1895) and the later ministries of Brown and his colleagues.[7]

SANCTIFICATION: NOT A DISTANT DREAM

Daniel Warner was seen by Charles Brown as having been active during the time between the expulsion of holiness teaching from the denominations and the rise of the new holiness denominations. Warner had embraced the doctrine of entire sanctification in 1877 and was himself expelled from his pulpit because of his holiness teaching. Brown also witnessed the decline of a focus of holiness in the twentieth century, even by heirs of the Holiness Movement. He judged that the

7. See Barry L. Callen, *It's God's Church! The Life and Legacy of Daniel Sidney Warner* (Anderson, IN: Warner Press, 1995).

doctrine of sanctification had been abused badly by many of its advocates and ridiculed thoroughly by many of its opponents. The tragic result was that few modern scholars cared to plunge into the welter of this supposed fanaticism. He would be an early and prominent exception to this neglect.

Following the 1944 release of his *The Meaning of Salvation*, Charles Brown proceeded in 1945 to write his pivotal volume *The Meaning of Sanctification*. At that time he was both editor of the *Gospel Trumpet* (Warner Press) and an associate professor of theology at Anderson College and Theological Seminary in Anderson, Indiana. With these books and ministry roles, he became a bridge between the late nineteenth-century holiness teachers and the holiness movements of the twentieth century.

The wisdom of Charles Brown is enduring. For example, although written in May of 1940, the following seems very contemporary: "We seem to live in an age where the caravans of Christianity are glad to rest, each in its little oasis of methods, budgets, building programs, and regular services—counting its gains in percentages, glad enough to break even, anxious to keep the goodwill of the public, fearful of violating any of the fine points of etiquette, and forgetting entirely the high calls of selfless service and deathless devotion which have hummed in the ears of all the great saints of the past."[8]

For Brown, becoming "saints" is a primary objective of the Christian faith. Brown was passionate about clarifying the meaning of Christian holiness and persistent about empha-

8. Charles E. Brown, "Objective of the Reformation," *Gospel Trumpet*, May 4, 1940.

sizing its importance for every Christian believer. Holiness must be more than a theory, a doctrine, a relic of church history, a distant dream.

This grand goal of experienced and expressed holiness, to which Brown so eloquently points, is no less crucial for today's churches. May this reissuing of Brown's *The Meaning of Sanctification* help open new doors of insight, commitment, spiritual attainment, Christian unity, and world evangelism.

Barry L. Callen
Editor of the
Wesleyan Theological Journal
and Aldersgate Press of the
Wesleyan/Holiness Consortium

PREFACE

That brilliant French theologian, Auguste Sabatier, crystallized in one sentence the substance of what I have tried to say in this book. "Salvation," he writes, "is deliverance from the power of evil, it is filial communion with God, which, restored to its proper place in the heart, henceforth becomes the spring of the believer's peace and joy, the true germ of eternal life, the victory of the Spirit."[1]

It was my first intention to discuss the whole subject of salvation in one book; but as I wrote, the manuscript grew to such dimensions that it seemed altogether best to publish the material in two volumes, separately titled and each complete in itself, and yet each complementary to the other. The first volume has been published under the title *The Meaning of Salvation;* this companion volume is now published under the title *The Meaning of Sanctification.*

The doctrine of sanctification has been abused so badly by its advocates and ridiculed so thoroughly by its opponents that few modern scholars care to plunge into the welter of fanaticism and passionate strife with which the subject is involved. To the present writer this seems a great pity and certain tragic loss. The subject of sanctification has ever been the holy of holies of the Christian church; and regardless of the method of obtaining this experience, it has always been esteemed a jewel in the breastplate of the church's high priest, our blessed Lord. And throughout all the church's nearly two thousand years of history there have always been pure and

1. Auguste Sabatier, *Religions of Authority,* p. 236.

radiant souls who rejoiced in the mystic light of a Shekinah that glows softly but brilliantly on the mercy seat within the sacred enclosure of the holy of holies. In every age there have been gentle souls filled with spiritual passion who have cherished this holy vision as the greatest treasure of life. Shall we Christians of the twentieth century leave that inner chamber not only silent, but empty, by reason of our neglect of the supreme purpose which Christ has always cherished regarding the relation of his people to himself?

The writer is one who believes in progress. The changing emphases of the church's teaching seem to him to be merely a reflection of the fact that the enduring church must interpret the eternal gospel in conformity with the changing needs and conditions of the world of our time. Doubtless it is a good thing that we are more active than our fathers were. There is a value in organization and co-operation. We prize the concept of the church as a corporate body of interacting individuals rather than a mob of selfish individualists who acknowledge no relation to each other. The Spirit of God is leading the church today as he led her nearly two thousand years ago. Nevertheless, it is still possible to overemphasize a good and necessary principle and in the process neglect an equally essential truth.

For this reason it will be a mistake if we neglect the inner experience of sanctification, which has inspired and strengthened the heartbeats of the church through all the ages past. Following this figure, we might think of a strong, healthy man so absorbed in his work that the strength of his heart seems not worthy of any attention. But let such a man develop a weakness of the heart, and he will find that no pressing task of his daily work is sufficiently important to take precedence over the task of repairing, rebuilding, and healing his heart, if that is any longer possible.

The doctrine of sanctification is for Christian people the most important of all the doctrines, because it teaches the way to find and to develop faith in Christ as the perfect healer of the heart, who alone can make it entirely well and fill it with the enduring strength of his Holy Spirit.

Let us, therefore, think of sanctification not as merely a wild and senseless debate upon matters of no importance, but rather as the completion of the work of redemption in the heart and soul of the believer. That is the thing of deepest interest to all earnest Christians.

It must also be remembered that while we of the church are devoting so much time to methods of Christian work, thousands of people are leaving the Christian faith and following cults, simply for the reason that the cults, by false doctrines, are emphasizing the soul culture and inner spiritual development which the church is well able to promote by a true doctrine of sanctification.

A word remains to be said regarding the method of developing this meaning. Scripture texts have been so twisted and misused in the past, and their application has been so perverted, that many intelligent Christians today seem to prefer a philosophical or psychological development of a religious subject, devoid of anything but the most casual allusion to pertinent Scripture texts. I find no fault with many helpful books which follow such a method, but I think that method is inadequate for the purpose of this book.

First of all, the Bible still lies at the foundation of all fruitful knowledge of God. Furthermore, nearly all earnest Christians reverence the Word of God with sincere hearts and find its sacred utterances to be the most helpful means of understanding the truth and planting the seeds of faith in the heart. It was a sound spiritual instinct which led the pioneers of the holiness movements to build with meticulous fidelity upon the very words of Holy Scripture.

While we have no superstitious belief in the Bible words as magical, we do have a pious reverence for them as sacred. We believe the saying of Jesus: "The words that I speak unto you, they are spirit, and they are life" (John 6:63). Generations of Christians have found this to be true. To quote these words of the Bible is a custom which will never go out of style in the true Zion of godly souls.

It would be a pity to try to teach the heights of Christian experience while neglecting the most useful of all means for the accomplishment of this purpose; namely, the healing, saving words of the gospel in the very language of the holy men of old time, who "spake as they were moved by the Holy Ghost." If the scoffers call this method a threshing of Scripture texts, reply can be made that by this threshing we come into possession of the wealth of the richest wheat in the land.

If this work were written for scholars, and if space allowed, it would be very profitable to analyze and expound separately the message of each Bible writer, especially those of the New Testament. But such a course lay beyond the purpose of this book, and I can only say that wherever Scripture texts have been used in a manner contrary to the popular interpretation I believe I have always followed sound, historical, and scientific methods of interpretation. In most, if not all, specific instances, reference can be made to the testimony of an able, modern scholar in confirmation of the view taken.

This book is not written to give battle, but to give light. If in parts issue is taken with the popular religious ideas of the day it is not through any lack of sympathy for the fundamental Christian tradition. I love that tradition and follow it with pious devotion, but that tradition is found in its truest form in the New Testament and in the writings of primitive Christianity before the days of Origen. The tradition which is rejected is a corruption of the original tradition which has forced itself upon our popular Christianity.

Nevertheless, the pure tradition of sanctification as taught in this volume has not been without its witnesses throughout the long history of the church. That tradition was gathered up and stated most clearly in modern times by John Wesley and his co-laborers in the great Wesleyan revival. They proved in one of the greatest laboratory experiments of church history that the doctrine of entire sanctification is not merely a dry, dead dogma useful only to furnish abundant matter for debate and church fights. On the contrary, they proved by practical demonstration that, personally experienced and witnessed by godly lives, this doctrine is most fruitful of personal, spiritual victory for the individual and of phenomenal growth and prosperity for the religious groups which hold to it in sincerity.

The practical value of the doctrine and experience of entire sanctification may be observed by noting a significant historical fact. Christianity made a greater expansion in the United States from 1790 to 1910 than it ever made anywhere else in any age or in any nation in a comparative period of time. The number of Christians increased in our nation during this time from 5 per cent to 43 per cent,[2] and this at a time when its population was expanding enormously.

The principal cause of this rapid religious growth was the vitalizing power of the doctrine and experience of entire sanctification as it leavened the whole lump of American Christianity through the Wesleyan revival.

The doctrine of entire sanctification is an heroic doctrine. It requires a spiritual church and ministry for its acceptance, promotion, development, and successful growth. It always tends to die out in a worldly church, but it will kindle a flame of fire in every community where it is accepted, witnessed to, and lived out in experience.

The very best of spiritual teaching cannot of itself give any person a religious experience. "Faith and love," says Clement of Alexandria, "are not taught. But knowledge conveyed from communication through the grace of God as a deposit, is entrusted to those who show themselves worthy of it; and from it the worth of love beams forth from light to light."[3]

The ablest Christian teachers of our time have for the most part given up all efforts to prove the fundamental truths

2. Kenneth Scott Latourette, *A History of the Expansion of Christianity,* Vol. IV: *The Great Century,* p. 177.

3. Clement, *The Stromata,* Book VII, chap. 10.

of the spiritual life. They believe with Blaise Pascal that "the heart hath its reasons which reason cannot know." For example, the writer believes firmly in democracy, but he realizes that it cannot be proved by logical, intellectual arguments to those who reject the fundamental postulates upon which it is built. We see, then, the amazing fact that multitudes of men have given their life for a truth which we of America hold with an iron grasp but which we cannot prove by reasoning to those who are unsympathetic.

Many truths as reasonable and as real as life itself cannot be proved by the rules of logic. We cannot prove the existence of music to those born deaf, nor the existence of the art of painting to those born blind. We cannot prove love to the hateful and unloving, and we cannot prove the doctrine of entire sanctification to doubters and scoffers. Regarding Luther, Harnack has made the observation that "he produced a complete confusion in religion for every one who approaches it from without."[4] And we might say the same of the doctrine of perfect love taught by the Wesleyan theologians.

No effort is made to *prove* sanctification. I have written for sincere Christians sympathetic with spiritual values and sensitive to them. For these I would remove fallacious intellectual obstacles which hitherto have prevented their seeking and finding this fullness of the blessing of the gospel of Christ. I have written also for those who would understand the experience better, both for their own enjoyment and to enable them to help others personally by leading them to Him "who shall sit as a refiner and purifier of silver" (Mal. 3:3).

4. Adolph Harnack, *History of Dogma,* Vol. VII, p. 202.

Those interested in a discussion of the truths concerning repentance, regeneration and the beginning of the Christian life are referred to my book *The Meaning of Salvation,* the companion volume of the present work.

The Meaning of Sanctification begins with a discussion of the theory of gradual sanctification. Next, the historical and scriptural evidences that millions of Christians have believed in a second crisis of salvation are traced. This crisis was experienced universally in the apostolic church. Then follows a study of the implications of such an experience and how to obtain it.

In appendices at the end of the book have been included some studies not deemed desirable to include in the body of the book.

This book has been written in the broken scraps of time saved from the pressing tasks of preaching, teaching, and editorial work. My only excuse for offering it in such imperfect condition is that the time is far spent, the night is at hand—that night when no man can work.

I have only these small loaves and fishes to offer the Master. May he multiply them as he did a like offering in another day.

As this simple spiritual meal is spread I would praise the beauty of holiness and raise one more voice in the song of the ages glorifying the "Lamb of God, which taketh away the sin of the world."

Yours in Christian service,
Charles Ewing Brown

I.
THE THEORY OF GRADUAL SANCTIFICATION

Perhaps it would not be an exaggeration to say that the average Christian of our own time has very hazy ideas about the nature and meaning of sanctification. As we have elsewhere pointed out, many thousands of Christians in America accept the Wesleyan doctrine of sanctification as a second work of grace. Christians who do not hold that doctrine generally have a confused mass of ideas and traditions which, when analyzed and formulated, may be seen to be based upon the historical doctrine of sanctification as set forth and expounded by the great Calvinistic theologians.

Probably the foremost of modern classics in this field is the *Systematic Theology* of Dr. Charles Hodge. Not within a hundred years has any theologian stated the historical position of Calvinism more ably than he. Therefore we take some space to set forth his views, because nearly every Christian doctrine of sanctification which opposes the Wesleyan theory will be found to rest upon Calvinistic theology; and an examination of the Calvinistic and anti-Wesleyan doctrine of sanctification will serve to disclose, along with the divergencies, areas of agreement in the doctrine of sanctification in Christian theology sometimes overlooked by those who discuss the doctrine merely in the light of current, popular sentimentalism.

Dr. Hodge gives voluminous treatment to the doctrine of sanctification, and it is necessary to shorten the quotations given somewhat; but this is done conscientiously, in the belief that direct reference to his works, available in all first-class theological libraries will show that he has not been misrepresented in the quotations cited. Dr. Hodge says:

> Sanctification in the Westminster Catechism is said to be the work of God's free grace, whereby we are renewed in the whole man after the image of God, and are enabled *more and more to die unto sin* and live unto righteousness.
>
> Agreeable to this definition, justification differs from sanctification, (1) in that the former is a transient act, the latter, a progressive work. (2) Justification is a forensic act, God acting as judge, declaring justice satisfied so far as the believing sinner is concerned, whereas sanctification is an effect due to the divine efficiency. (3) Justification changes, or declares to be changed, the relation of the sinner to the justice of God; sanctification involves a change of character. (4) The former, therefore, is objective, the latter subjective. (5) The former is founded on what Christ has

done for us; the latter is the effect of what He does in us. (6) Justification is complete and the same in all, while *sanctification is progressive, and is more complete in some than in others.*[1]

Admitting sanctification to be a supernatural work, the question still remains, What does it consist in? What is the nature of the effect produced? The truth which lies at the foundation of all the scriptural representations of this subject is, that regeneration, the quickening, of which believers are the subject, while it involves the implanting, or communication of a new principle or form of life, *does not effect the immediate and entire deliverance of the soul from all sin.* A man raised from the dead may be and long continue to be, in a very feeble, diseased, and suffering state. So the soul by nature dead in sin, may be quickened together with Christ, and *not be rendered thereby perfect.* The principle of life may be very feeble, *it may have much in the soul uncongenial with its nature, and the conflict between the old and the next life may be protracted and painful.* Such not only may be, but *such in fact is the case in all the ordinary experience of the people of God.* Here we find one of the characteristic and far-reaching differences between the Romish and Protestant systems, nothing of the nature of sin remains in the soul after regeneration as effected in baptism. From this the theology of the Church of Rome deduces its doctrine of the merit

1. Charles Hodge, *Systematic Theology*, Vol III, p. 213. (Italics are the author's.)

of good works; of perfection; of works of supererogation; and, indirectly, those of absolution and indulgences. But according to the Scriptures, the universal experience of Christians, and the undeniable evidence of history, *regeneration does not remove all sin.* The Bible is filled with the record of *the inward conflicts* of the most eminent of the servants of God, with their falls, their backslidings, their repentings, and their lamentations over their continued shortcomings. And not only this, but the *nature of the conflict between good and evil in the heart of the renewed is fully described,* the contending principles are distinguished and designated, and the necessity, difficulties, and perils of the struggle, as well as the method of properly sustaining it, are set forth repeatedly and in detail. In the seventh chapter of the Epistle to the Romans we have an account of this conflict elaborately described by the Apostle as drawn from his own experience. And the same thing occurs in Galatians 5:16-17: "This I say then, walk in the Spirit, and ye shall not fulfill the lust of the flesh. For the flesh lusteth against the Spirit, and the Spirit against the flesh: and these are contrary the one to the other: so that ye cannot do the things that ye would." Again, in Ephesians 6:10-18, in view of the conflict which the believer has to sustain with the evils of his own heart and with the powers of darkness, the Apostle exhorts his brethren to be strong in the Lord, and in the power of his might...."Wherefore take unto you the whole armor of God, that ye may be able to withstand in the evil day, and having done all, to stand."

With the teachings of the Scriptures the experience of Christians in all ages and in all parts of the Church agrees. Their writings are filled with the account of their *struggles with the remains of sin in their own hearts;* with confessions; with prayers for divine aid; and with longings after the final victory over all evil, which is to be experienced only in heaven. The great lights of the Latin Church, the Augustines and Bernards and Fenélons, were humble, penitent, struggling believers, even to the last, and with Paul did not regard themselves as having already attained, or as being already perfect. And what the Bible and Christian experience prove to be true, history puts beyond dispute. Either there is no such thing as regeneration in the world, or *regeneration does not remove all sin from those who are its subjects.*

Putting Off the Old, and Putting On the New Man

Such being the foundation of the scriptural representations concerning sanctification, its nature is thereby determined. As all men since the fall are in a state of sin, not only sinners because guilty of specific acts of transgression, *but also as depraved,* their nature perverted and corrupted, regeneration is the *infusion of a new principle of life* in this corrupt nature. It is *leaven introduced* to diffuse its influence gradually through the whole mass. *Sanctification, therefore, consists in two things: first, the removing more and more the principles of evil still infecting our nature,* and destroying their power; and secondly, the growth of the principle of spiritual life until it controls the thoughts, feelings, and acts, and brings the soul into the image of Christ....

What Romans 7:7-25 Teaches

Assuming, then, that we have in this chapter an account of the experience of a true and even of an advanced Christian, we learn that in every Christian there is a mixture of good and evil; that *the original corruption of nature is not entirely removed by regeneration;* that although the believer is made a new creature, is translated from the kingdom of darkness into the kingdom of God's dear Son, he is but partially sanctified; that his selfishness, pride, discontent, worldliness, still cleave to, and torment him, that they effectually prevent his "doing what he would," *they prevent his living without sin,* they prevent his intercourse with God being as intimate and uninterrupted as he could and does desire. He finds not only that he is often, even daily, overcome so as to sin in thought, word, and deed, but also that his faith, love, zeal, and devotion are never such as to satisfy his own conscience; much less can they satisfy God. He therefore is daily called upon to confess, repent, and pray for forgiveness. The Apostle designates these conflicting principles which he found within himself, the one, *indwelling sin; "sin that dwelleth in me";* or the *"law in my members";* "the *law of sin";* the other, *"the mind," "the law of my mind," "the inward man."*

We learn, further, that the control of the evil principle is resisted, that subjection to it is regarded as a hateful bondage, that the good principle is in the main victorious, and that through Christ it will ultimately be completely triumphant. Sanctification therefore, according to this representation, consists in the gradual triumph of the new nature implanted in regeneration over the evil that still remains after the heart is renewed. In other words, as elsewhere expressed, it is a dying unto sin and living unto righteousness (I Pet. 2:24).

Perfectionism

Protestant Doctrine

The doctrine of Lutherans and Reformed, the two great branches of the Protestant Church, is, that *sanctification is never perfected in this life;* that *sin is not in any case entirely subdued;* so that the most advanced believer has need as long as he continues in the flesh, daily to pray for the forgiveness of sins....

God has in Christ made provision for the complete salvation of his people: that is, for their entire deliverance from the penalty of the law, from the power of sin, from all sorrow, pain, and death; and not only for mere negative deliverance, but for their being transformed into the image of Christ, filled with his Spirit, and glorified by the beauty of the Lord. It is, however, too plain that, unless sanctification be an exception, no one of these promises, besides that which concerns justification, is perfectly fulfilled in this life. *Justification does not admit of degrees.* A man either is under condemnation, or he is not. And, therefore, from the nature of the case, *justification is instantaneous and complete* [Why is not sanctification the same?][2], as soon as the sinner believes. But the question is, whether when God promises to make his people perfectly holy, perfectly happy, and perfectly glorious, He thereby promises to make them perfect in holiness in this life? If the promises of happiness and glory are not perfectly fulfilled in this life, why should the promise of sanctification be thus fulfilled? [This is confusing the happiness and glory of heaven with the privilege of salvation from sin in this life, repeatedly promised in the New Testament.]

Passages Which Describe the Conflict Between the Flesh and the Spirit

More definitely is this truth taught in those passages which describe the conflict in the believer between the flesh and the Spirit. To this reference has already been made. That the seventh chapter of Paul's Epistle to the Romans is an account of his own inward life at the time of writing that Epistle, has already, as it is believed, been sufficiently proved; and such has been the belief of the great body of evangelical Christians in all ages of the Church. If this be the correct interpretation of that passage, then it proves that Paul, at least, was not free from sin; that he had to contend with a law in

2. Brackets indicate comments by the author, Charles E. Brown.

his members, warring against the law of his mind; that he groaned constantly under the burden of indwelling sin. At a still later period of his life, when he was just ready to be offered up, he says to the Philippians (3:12-14), "Not as though I had already attained, either were already perfect: but I follow after, if that I may apprehend that for which also I am apprehended of Christ Jesus. Brethren, I count not myself to have apprehended: but this one thing I do, forgetting those things which are behind and reaching forth unto those things which are before, I press toward the mark for the prize of the high calling of God in Christ Jesus." [The Apostle was not here denying his present attainment of full salvation. He was opposing the heresy of such men as Hymenaeus and Philetus, "who concerning the truth have erred, saying that the resurrection is past already" (II Tim. 2:18). Paul denies that he has attained to the perfection of bodily resurrection. For a fuller discussion of all such passages see my book *The Meaning of Salvation.*] This is an unmistakable declaration on the part of the Apostle that even at this late period of his life he was not yet perfect; he had not attained the end of perfect conformity to Christ, but was pressing forward, as one in a race, with all earnestness that he might reach the end of his calling. To answer this, as has been done by some distinguished advocates of perfectionism, by saying that Paul's not being perfect is no proof that other men may not be is not very satisfactory.

The parallel passage in Galatians (5:16-26) is addressed to Christians generally. It recognizes the fact that they are imperfectly sanctified; that in them the renewed principle, the Spirit as the source of spiritual life, is in conflict with the flesh, the remains of their corrupt nature. It exhorts them to mortify the flesh (not the body, but their corrupt nature) and to strive constantly to walk under the controlling influence of the Spirit. The characteristic difference between the unrenewed and the renewed is not that the former are entirely sinful, and the latter perfectly holy; but that the former are wholly under the control of their fallen nature, while the latter have the Spirit of God dwelling in them, which leads them to crucify the flesh, and to strive after complete conformity to the image of God. There was nothing in the character of the Galatian Christians to render this exhortation applicable to them alone. What the Scriptures teach concerning faith, repentance, and justification, is intended for all Christians; and so what is taught of sanctification suits the case of all believers. Indeed, if a man thinks himself perfect, and apprehends that he has already attained what his fellow believers are only striving for, a great part of the Bible must for him lose its value. What use can he make of the Psalms, the vehicle through which the people of God for millenniums have poured out their hearts? How can such a man sympathize with Ezra, Nehemiah, or any of the prophets? How strange to him must be the language of Isaiah, "Woe is me! for

> I am undone; because I am a man of unclean lips, and I dwell in the midst of a people of unclean lips: for mine eyes have seen the King, the LORD of hosts."[3]

These extensive quotations have been given because they state far more forcefully than the average opponent of the Wesleyan doctrine of sanctification ever could present the arguments against entire sanctification as obtainable in this life. Moreover, this Calvinistic doctrine is certified as orthodox for all of that faith by the verdict of the *Westminster Confession,* which reads as follows:

> They who are effectually called and regenerated, having a new heart and a new spirit created in them, *are further sanctified,* really and personally, through the virtue of Christ's death and resurrection, by his Word and Spirit dwelling in them; the dominion of the whole *body of sin is destroyed,* and the several lusts thereof are more and more weakened and mortified, and they more and more quickened and strengthened, in all saving graces, to the practice of true holiness, without which no man shall see the Lord.
>
> 2. This sanctification is throughout in the whole man, *yet imperfect in this life;* there *abideth still some remnants of corruption in every part,* whence ariseth a continual and *irreconcilable war,* the *flesh lusting against* the spirit, and the spirit against the flesh.

3. Ibid., pp. 220-221, 223-224, 245-249. (Italics are the author's.)

> 3. In which war, although the remaining corruption for a time may much prevail, yet, through the continual supply of strength from the sanctifying Spirit of Christ, the regenerate part doth overcome; and so the saints grow in grace, perfecting holiness in the fear of God."[4]

Likewise, that entire creed indicates the moment when all inbred sin is to be eradicated from the heart of the believer. That moment is at the instant of death. "The souls of the righteous, being then made perfect in holiness, are received into the highest heavens, where they behold the face of God in light and glory."[5]

If anyone should object to being represented by Dr. Hodge and the *Westminster Confession,* we can only say that these documents represent the ablest presentation of the most widely held of all anti-Wesleyan Christian doctrines of sanctification. We are not interested in any anti-Christian discussion of sanctification, but only in studying the question from a Christian viewpoint.

A DOCTRINE OF ANTI-SANCTIFICATION

Accepting these authorities, then, as valid representatives of the Christian anti-Wesleyan doctrine of sanctification, we must reply that this is not a doctrine of sanctification, but rather of anti-sanctification. As we study the Calvinistic theory of gradual sanctification we are reminded of a charac-

4. *The Westminster Confession of Faith,* chap. 13.
5. Ibid., chap. 32.

ter in ancient Greek mythology, Sisyphus, who in Hades was condemned to roll up a hill a great stone which constantly rolled back, making his task incessant; and if there ever was an incessant task of achieving sanctification it is the one set by Calvinism that assures a man that even if he should have sixty years of effort before him and that if he should do his utmost he would, notwithstanding, never be free from sin until the moment of his death.

At the same time, a young man converted at the age of sixteen, who was entirely ignorant of the doctrine of gradual sanctification would, if he died, say within six months, be just as completely and fully sanctified as the man who had striven for the attainment of the experience throughout sixty years. What we object to here is the confusion of two conceivable methods of obtaining the experience. If sanctification is a gift from God, then the sixteen-year-old convert, who had been saved only six months, may seem to have a logical right to this gift as much as the veteran saint of many years. But that right would be based upon the experience as a gift from God. On the contrary, if it is something which a man works out for himself by long and painful effort, surely there is something incongruous in thinking that he will have no more gains for his pains in sixty years of struggle than a youth would have in six months of making practically no effort at all to that end. Merely to contemplate these facts is to assure a reasonable mind that sanctification is not an attainment. It is not something for which a man works; it is a gift. It is not a thing that a man *grows into; it is a given thing, which he receives.*

Dr. Hodge gives this whole argument away when he admits that sanctification is supernatural and comes by faith. It is impossible to combine gradual sanctification with the doctrine of sanctification by faith. Gradual sanctification fits in well with the doctrine of works. It might be presumed to come as a reward for long service in the kingdom, but as Paul has said, "to him that worketh is the reward not reckoned of grace, but of debt" (Rom. 4:4). If a Christian is sanctified as the reward of long striving against inward sin, then he receives the payment of a debt which God owes him, and his reward is not of grace nor of faith. These two methods will not mix. This doctrine of sanctification by works is a denial of the whole principle of salvation by faith.

WORK WITHOUT PAY

While the Calvinistic doctrine of sanctification achieved gradually by hard and toilsome effort is a denial of the principle of salvation by faith, it has a further defect. The attainment of the reward of sanctification bears no proper logical relation to the amount of effort which the seeker puts forth in order to obtain it. The sixteen-year-old convert who died six months after his conversion obtained entire sanctification entirely as fully and as completely as the aged saint who worked at the task for sixty years. Surely sanctification is not by works, or the veteran saint would not have to do a thousand times more to receive it than the youthful Christian. And remember that the veteran saint does not receive one iota more of holiness and sanctification than the youthful

Christian who died in the first flush of his conversion. Both received exactly the same boon of entire sanctification.

THE DOCTRINE OF GRADUAL SANCTIFICATION DEMANDS PURGATORY

These considerations show that the moment of death as the end of the process of sanctification and the exact time of its obtainment is chosen purely for dogmatic reasons. The doctrine is shaped in this form merely to avoid the Roman Catholic dogma of purgatory. Had it not been for a radical antipathy to that doctrine, Calvinists would have followed the logic of their position and would have said that the accomplishment of the work of entire sanctification would require a certain amount of effort and toil. If that toil is completed before death, then a man will be sanctified possibly twenty or thirty years before his death. If, on the contrary, it is not accomplished at the moment of his death then it will be finished in purgatory after possibly hundreds of years of suffering and painful toil. Mind, I do not say that this is Calvinistic doctrine; but rather that the presuppositions of the theory call for it and that the logical development of the doctrine was prevented from coming to maturity by opposition to the doctrine of purgatory. In other words, the Calvinistic doctrine of sanctification by works requires a purgatory to make it consistent and logical.

Now we of the Wesleyan school oppose the doctrine of purgatory as much as the Calvinists do, but we have a doctrine of sanctification which teaches that the remains of sin in believers are not eradicated by long labor and toil, but are destroyed in one crisis-experience of active faith in the moment when the soul is baptized with the Holy Ghost and with power.

Christians must take their choice, unless indeed they deny the historic teachings of Protestantism and assert that there is no inbred sin in believers and therefore entire sanctification is accomplished at the moment of conversion. This theory is not only unscriptural, it is also contrary to experience and observation as applied to the lives of Christians.

II.
INDICATIONS OF A SECOND CRISIS

Against the theory held by the Calvinists let us place the scriptural doctrine of a second crisis, in which entire sanctification is realized in one dramatic baptism of the Holy Ghost and of power that destroys all the remains of carnality and fills the believer with all the fullness of God.

THE PAGES OF ROCK

It is interesting to stand on the rim of the Grand Canyon and study the various strata of rock that have been laid down there throughout the course of ages. Here, and elsewhere in the Rocky Mountain district, one is impressed with the complexity of the geological record. An unsympathetic observer might jump to the conclusion that God wrote the story of geological development in shorthand quite indifferent to man's ability to read it. In fact, those mighty leaves of rock lay there as a closed book for ages of time and only in recent years have they been read by the diligent study of devoted scientists. Evidently, God was not careless of the readers of his geological book, but he did not insult their intelligence by making it too easy. In that ancient rock book is laid down the record of mighty upheavals of the earth's crust, gigantic clefts broken through miles of solid rock. Such was the condition at one time where now all is still as the hands of the dead. Likewise, there are written in the ancient records of the Christian church various indications of the mighty earthquake and volcanic outbursts of spiritual power in the hearts and lives of those early saints. It all reposes calm and simple in the history of the church, but diligent students can see the marks of a great experience little known and observed in our own day.

THE CEREMONY OF CONFIRMATION AS EVIDENCE

A ceremony universal in the Roman Catholic Church, and quite common in the older ritualistic churches, is called confirmation. This ceremony of confirmation is just as important a theological fossil, and in its own way means as much to the thoughtful Christian, as an ancient fossil in the rocks means to a geological student. It is evident that some of the Protestant communions have merely imitated the Catholic ceremony without attaching the same meaning to it as does the Roman church. Therefore we shall study the Roman Catholic ceremony as being the older, both in form and meaning.

This so-called sacrament has several names, such as confirmation, the seal, the anointing, or the laying on of hands. In the Roman Catholic Church it is always administered by the bishop, or a priest authorized by him, to young baptized children old enough to have finished their catechism and to receive their first communion.

The principal feature of the ceremony is the anointing with the consecrated oil. After prayer the bishop makes the sign of the cross on the forehead of the candidate and says in Latin, "I seal thee with the sign of the cross, and confirm thee with the oil of salvation, in the name of the Father, the Son, and of the Holy Ghost." However, the Greek form is undoubtedly much older and in it the bishop says, "The seal of the gift of the Holy Spirit (is imparted to thee)." "Its effect," says C. Weizsacker, "is the communication of the Holy Spirit, and equipment for the battle of life."

There is such a mass of definite evidence in the ancient literature of the church as to amount to positive proof that the ceremony of confirmation is a continuation in ritual form of the New Testament custom of laying hands upon young converts and praying for them to be filled with the Holy Spirit, as a second crisis in salvation, an experience subsequent to baptism and hence subsequent to regeneration. (See Heb. 6:2; Acts 19:6; 8:12-19.) Further connection is noted between this rite and the unction of I John 2:27, the anointing of II Corinthians 1:21, and the sealing of II Corinthians 1:22; Ephesians 1:13; 4:30.

The famous African Church Father Tertullian, who died about AD 230, undoubtedly believed in baptismal regeneration. He says that "in the water, under (the witness of) the angel, we are cleansed, and prepared *for* the Holy Spirit." Then he goes on to say, "Thus, too, does the angel, the witness of baptism, make the paths straight for the Holy Spirit, who is about to come upon us" and continues: "After this, when we have issued from the font [of baptism], we are thoroughly anointed with the blessed unction."[1] He likens this unction to the anointing of priests in the Old Testament. "In the next place the hand is laid on us, invoking and inviting the Holy Spirit through benediction....Then, over our cleansed and blessed bodies willingly descends from the Father that Holiest Spirit." He likens this coming of the Spirit on the newly baptized to the coming of the dove upon Christ. "So by the self-same law of heavenly effect, to earth—that is, to our flesh—as it emerges from the font, after its old sins, flies the *dove* of the Holy Spirit, bringing us the peace of God, sent out from the heavens."[2]

In another place Tertullian distinguishes very sharply between salvation and the baptism of the Holy Spirit as a second work of grace. He is pleading, like the great lawyer that he was, the value of the human body and why it was not unworthy of resurrection at the last day. "The flesh," he says, "indeed, is washed, in order that the soul may be cleansed." Here he referred to regeneration in the act of baptism.

"The flesh is anointed, that the soul may be consecrated." This refers to the anointing with the chrism after baptism, showing that consecration follows conversion. "The flesh is

1. Tertullian, *On Baptism*, chap. 7.

2. Ibid., chap. 8.

signed (with the cross), that the soul too may be fortified; the flesh is shadowed with the imposition of hands that the soul also may be illuminated by the spirit."[3]

The fact that Tertullian believed in baptismal regeneration reveals that sacramentalism had made inroads upon the church in his time; that does not by any means disprove our doctrine, but rather confirms it. Everything had been reduced to ritual and form, but it is important to remember that when this crystallization took place regeneration and the baptism of the Spirit were still separated into two distinct experiences, which normally took place in close connection with each other but in a definite order of time: first, regeneration; next, the baptism of the Spirit. If regeneration takes place in a mechanical ceremony, so does sanctification, or Spirit baptism. If we believe that the regeneration of which Tertullian wrote must be purely a work of the Spirit and that his conception of it was too mechanical, then we must say the same thing of the baptism of the Spirit of which he wrote; but however he may have misunderstood the inner meaning of these rites, one thing is certain—he clearly grasped the fact that the baptism of the Spirit is subsequent to regeneration and to water baptism. In other words, the leaders of the church in that age were not any more mechanical about the reception of the baptism of the Spirit than they were concerning regeneration itself.

As we have shown that at a very early time consecration was symbolized by anointing the baptized believer with oil, Theophilus of Antioch, in the latter part of the second century, traces the name "Christian" from the chrism, or anointing,

3. Tertullian, *On the Resurrection of the Flesh*, p. 551.

which believers received at the moment of their reception of the Spirit. He thinks that it is very necessary for Christians to have this anointing for the conflicts of life, just as the athletes of that day anointed their bodies with oil for their athletic contests.

Cyprian, the great bishop of Carthage in the early part of the third century, said concerning the baptism of the Spirit: "For they who had believed in Samaria had believed with a true faith; and within, in the Church which is one, and to which alone it is granted to bestow the grace of baptism and to remit sins, had been baptized by Philip the deacon, whom the same apostles had sent. And therefore, because they had obtained legitimate and ecclesiastical baptism, there was no need that they should be baptized any more, but only that which was needed was performed by Peter and John; viz., that prayer being made for them, and hands being imposed, the Holy Spirit should be invoked and poured out upon them, which now, too, is done among us, so that they who are baptized in the Church are brought to the prelates of the Church, and by our prayers and by the imposition of hands obtain the Holy Spirit, and are perfected with the Lord's seal.[4]

"Imposition of hands and confirmation confer something on him that is born again and regenerated in Christ."[5]

"It is not all one to obtain remission of sins and to receive such power."[6]

4. *The Epistles of Cyprian,* LXXII, to Jubaianus.

5. Eusebius Emesemus, "Sermon on Pentecost" (middle of the fourth century).

6. Chysostom, Homily XVIII (latter part of the fourth century).

Augustine, greatest theologian of the ancient church, wrote: "In propriety of speech neither the apostles nor any other man but Christ alone as He is God, could give the Holy Ghost; for the apostles only laid hands on men that the Holy Ghost by their prayers might descend on them; which custom the church now observed and practiced by her bishops and governors also."[7]

Again he writes, commenting on Acts 2:37-38: "In the Church truly in which was the Holy Ghost, were both brought to pass, that is, both the remission of sins, and the receiving of the gift."[8]

After infant baptism came in, it was regarded as unsuitable to perform the ceremony of confirmation on infants, for it would indicate that they had received the sanctifying baptism of the Holy Spirit. Therefore this part of the baptismal rites was removed and set up as a second separate sacrament to be imparted to children and youths old enough to understand something of its meaning. The very fact that this separation was made is of itself evidence that the church always believed two separate experiences of the Christian life were signified by these rites.[9]

THE LAYMEN AND THE PERFECT IN THE NEW TESTAMENT

The average indifferent Christian is quite unaware that all the elements of the gospel are essentially matters of faith. They are not physical substances lying around open to the view of

7. Augustine, *On the Trinity,* Book XV, chap. 26.
8. Augustine, Sermon 21.
9. J. Gilchrist Lawson, *Deeper Experiences of Famous Christians.*

saint and sinner alike. They are like the elements of art, music, mathematics, and advanced science—realities which reveal their inner meaning only to those who seek it with sympathetic appreciation and diligent research. One can point out to an ignorant man an obscure feature of rock formation and tell him what the geologists understand it to mean, and he will ridicule the whole exposition. It means nothing to him, because he does not possess the scientific background that makes the argument appeal to the scientist. In the same way we are aware that there are obscure points in the New Testament which the spiritually indifferent will pass over without noticing at all and the dogmatic opposer will ridicule as having no relevancy. Yet even many of these obscure points of Scripture will have a deep meaning for the sensitive, spiritually minded Christian who has no dogmatic bias against learning all the truth as rapidly as possible.

One of these obscure points is the existence of two words in the Greek New Testament which in English mean, roughly, "laymen" and "perfect." In his great work on the *History of Primitive Christianity* J. Weiss devotes a long passage to these two terms. The passage is altogether too long to quote here, but any reader who is interested may find it, beginning in volume II, page 624. Not to be too technical, it seems necessary to specify the Greek word *idiotai* (I Cor. 14:16, 23-24). In each place in this fourteenth chapter the word is translated "unlearned." In Acts 4:13 the same term is translated "ignorant." It is clear that the translators of the Authorized Version, having neither the experience nor the scholarship to fathom these passages, were deeply perplexed as to how to translate them. The word has the general meaning of "lower class," depending upon the connection. If the class is professional, then the *idiotai* are the unskilled; in some cases "laymen" would describe them. The professional teachers of Jerusalem did not necessarily mean that the Apostles were ignorant men, but that they were not skilled professionally.

The term was used to distinguish the mass membership of a group from the gifted leadership. Weiss believes that *idiotai* was applied to those who did not possess the Spirit.

In contrast to these imperfect Christians, Christians of the lower grade, there occurs repeated mention of the perfect *teleios.* The following are passages where this term occurs in the Epistles and the English word which is used to translate it in the Authorized Version: I Cor. 2:6, "perfect"; 14:20, "men"; Eph. 4:13, "perfect man"; Phil. 3:15, "perfect"; Col. 1:28, "perfect"; 4:12, "perfect"; Heb. 5:14, "of full age"; Jas. 3:2, "perfect man." These passages refer to Christians as perfect.

Paul sometimes held meetings with these "perfect" Christians separately from the whole church (I Cor. 2:6; I Cor. 14:23). These perfect Christians are identified with the *pneumatika,* or "spiritual," Christians. Following are the passages wherein *pneumatikos* is applied to Christians in the New Testament. It is always translated "spiritual" (I Cor. 2:15; 3:1; 14:37; Gal. 6:1). Here is a notable and neglected layer of New Testament truth laid open to the contemplation of the reverent student. Two classes of believers are clearly distinguished in the New Testament church. The difference between them was that one group did not have the gift of the Spirit and the other one did have that gift, which made them "spiritual" and "perfect."

Some kind of distinction between believers continued permanently in the history of the church. Clement of Alexandria (d. AD 215) makes a distinction between the lower stage of Christian character experienced by the ordinary believer and the higher life.

Describing the theology of Clement, Dr. George P. Fisher, the church historian, writes: "The regenerated life begins in baptism. It includes the forgiveness of sins. Henceforward there is a *twofold possibility.* There is a *lower* stage of Christian character, that of the *ordinary believer* who attains to holiness under the influence of fear and hope; and there is the *higher life,* where *fear is cast out by love.* Simply to be saved is something very different from salvation in the nobler sense."[10]

It is not necessary to subscribe to all the details of Clement's doctrine of Christian perfection to see in him a continuation of the persistent Christian tradition that there is a higher life for believers, a second crisis in redemption. This higher life is lived by the "true gnostic" (from *gnosis,* knowledge), who knows spiritual things in the manner pointed out by John, "Ye have an unction from the Holy One, and ye know all things....The same anointing teacheth you of all things, and is truth, and is no lie" (I John 2:20, 27).

In later years the distinction between the higher and lower Christian life was drawn between the clergy and the laity. At another time the monastic life professed to be superior, and during the Middle Ages the mystics laid claim to a higher experience. Nevertheless, throughout all the church's history, the memory of the perfect Christians of the New Testament

10. George P. Fisher, *History of Christian Doctrine,* p. 96.

has continually spurred the ordinary Christian to lofty aspiration. It is for us to ask, Is that aspiration vain?

THE CLOUD OF MANY WITNESSES

While not many orthodox Christians would agree with Schliermacher in his efforts to construct a systematic theology out of Christian experience alone, it is reasonable to appeal to Christian experience as an aid in interpreting the Scriptures. Of course, the main source of information regarding all Christian experience except our own is, of necessity, testimony. Please note carefully that we do not believe that any amount of testimony could overthrow or nullify the plain teachings of the Word of God, but we do believe that a vast mass of testimony of experience—not theory—should have some weight in interpreting an otherwise obscure point.

If Christian testimony is to be allowed any such weight, then it appears that the general principle of a second crisis in Christian experience must demand consideration from all thoughtful Christians. First of all, there are the holiness people in America and throughout the world. We could not pretend to count them—truly they are known only to God—but their number must amount to millions in the aggregate; for they are found everywhere, not only in the holiness churches, but also sprinkled widely among the other denominations. True, we might cut their numbers down appreciably by applying rigorous standards of criticism in an effort to distinguish between those with original experiences and others who are only imitators. In thinking of such tests, however, it is only fair to consider how much the ranks of conventional Christianity in general would be thinned by such a process.

Remembering that modern people began professing this second crisis under the preaching of the Wesleys far back in the eighteenth century, it is evident that literally millions of earnest, sincere Christians have devoutly believed that by faith they entered into a second rest after regeneration.[11] While we do not deny that they could have been mistaken, yet, recalling the heroic vigor of their experience of Christ's love, one is more likely to ask, Are we not in danger of making a mistake by neglecting the very element of their experience to which they attributed their spiritual power?

In thinking of the exponents of a second crisis we must also list the Keswick Conference Movement. This is a movement in the British Isles in which Christians of all denominations, including some notable church leaders, great scholars, and Anglican bishops, participate. While these people do not interpret the second crisis in the way that we do, especially with regard to inbred sin, they may honestly be counted as witnesses to a second crisis in Christian experience, a baptism of the Holy Spirit subsequent to regeneration which definitely initiates the justified believer into the wealth and joy of a victorious Christian life. While we wish the Keswick people were able to interpret this experience as we do, nevertheless, we rejoice that they have discovered the principal point upon which we insist—there is a rest for the people of God subsequent to conversion.

11. Cf. J. Gilchrist Lawson, *Op. cit.*

WHERE THE SAINTS HAVE TROD

Not the holiness people of the Keswickites alone have made this discovery. The Christian mystics of the Middle Ages, although intellectually confused by the tradition, superstitions, and philosophy of their time, did rise into the clear atmosphere of true perfection from a spiritual standpoint.

In this connection it is interesting to note that a good case can be made out to prove that nearly every one of the great evangelists and Christian workers of modern time, and even of all times so far as the records are available, came to a definite point where he entered into a deeper experience of the grace of God by some dramatic and epochal crisis. E. Stanley Jones is an outstanding example of this. Some of these men have even preached against entire sanctification as a theory, but they have had an experience of it in their lives. Prof. William James has gathered many testimonies in his book *Varieties of Religious Experience.* While some of these testimonies are plainly examples of abnormal or deranged minds, and they are all laid out by James with the coldness of a scientist examining insect specimens, nevertheless, in many of them there is such a warmth and spiritual reality that even the professor himself is compelled to acknowledge that these people have touched supernatural sources of power.

The Quakers have preached a form of this doctrine for many generations. In 1675 Robert Barclay wrote fifteen propositions which were universally accepted by the Friends as expressing their beliefs (although the Friends do not officially recognize any binding standards of doctrine). The Eighth Proposition reads as follows:

In whom this holy and pure birth is fully brought forth the body of death and sin comes to be crucified and removed, and their hearts united and subjected unto the truth, so as not to obey any suggestions or temptation of the evil one, but to be free from actual sinning and transgressing of the law of God, and in that respect perfect. Yet doth this perfection still admit of a growth; and there remaineth a possibility of sinning where the mind doth not most diligently and watchfully attend unto the Lord.[12]

12. Philip Schaff, *Creeds of Christendom,* Vol. III, pp. 794-795.

III.
THE SYMBOLISM OF THE OLD TESTAMENT

The pioneers of the holiness movement preached the doctrine of entire sanctification with unflagging zeal. Part of the evidences for this truth they drew from the symbolism of the Old Testament. Of recent years there has been some hesitation regarding this type of evidence concerning the doctrine of entire sanctification. In general, there has been a feeling that it is improper, as they say, to "allegorize" the Old Testament in this way and thus use its historical data as proof of an obscure doctrine. This reaction against the symbolism of the Old Testament has been carried entirely too far, as many critical scholars now believe.[1]

1. See Darwell Stone, "The Mystical Interpretation of the Old Testament," in *A New Commentary on Holy Scriptures*, p. 688.

The point is not whether man today using his own imagination is free to spiritualize the Old Testament so as to prove whatever comes to his mind; modern criticism has definitely ruled against any such frivolous twisting of the ancient scriptures. The simple fact is: The New Testament writers in general, and the Apostle Paul in particular, did allegorize, or as we say, "spiritualize," the historical material of the Old Testament; and if we reject the ideas which they developed in this way, we must deny a large part of the New Testament and reject its teachings.

This is a fact so plain that no scholar would need any evidence to support it, but since we are not all scholars let us refer to J. A. Weiss. He says that Paul "used this method (I Cor. 9:9; 10:5; Gal. 4:21-31), but not nearly to the same extent as we find it used in the Epistle to the Hebrews for instance."[2]

Now if the writers of the New Testament allegorized the historical stories of the Old Testament, and if we refuse to accept their results, then we must willfully shut our eyes to much truth which the New Testament has to show us.

Bearing these facts in mind, I feel free to assert that those parts of the Old Testament which are definitely allegorized by New Testament writers may well be called "types" without fear of violating some rationalistic rule of criticism. This sound critical method opens the door for us into some very striking truths reflected in the Book of Hebrews.

2. Cf. Johannes Weiss, *The History of Primitive Christianity*, Vol. I, p. 335.

THE REST THAT REMAINETH FOR GOD'S PEOPLE

It would make this book far too long if the writer should do all the work for the reader. To condense as much as possible, let the student read the fourth chapter of the Book of Hebrews. This study is worth a day of any Christian's time. There he will learn that the world was made in six ages of time. The seventh age began at the close of creation and is continuing to the present moment. It is God's day of rest.

Since it was impossible for the Israelite as a natural man to rest forever in the flesh, one day in seven was given to him as a type of the eternal rest of the soul. As God's rest was symbolized, or typified, by the Jewish Sabbath, that Jewish Sabbath was a type of the rest of God into which the soul enters when, perfectly purged and cleansed from all carnality and truly infilled with the Holy Ghost, it finds the rest that "remaineth for the people of God." The recurring rest of the seventh day in the Old Testament was a reflection of the partial experience of the regenerated Christian who rests and yet not completely. The perfect rest is the rest of the entirely sanctified who enter into the place of victory where struggle and labor are forever ended. Proof that this is an experience possible for Christians today is found in the exhortation "to enter into that rest" (Heb. 4:11). This is sufficient evidence that that rest is not heaven alone but is an experience obtainable in this life; because no one would be exhorted to make a special effort to enter the final heaven by any act of his own will—that must await the moment of death. Voluntarily to hasten it is to commit suicide.

HEAVEN ON EARTH BEGUN

However, we are not ranging into the ecstatic rhapsody of the mystics when we say that it is the plain teaching of the New Testament that Christians may attain to the heavenly state here on earth. The works of the most radical, critical scholars have admitted as much, as can be proved by numerous citations. An illustration of this truth is found in Revelation 21:2, a passage that has perplexed Bible students for nearly two thousand years. It cannot be lifted out of the clouds of confusion until its Platonic background is understood. Platonism taught that there is in heaven a pattern of everything that exists on earth. In his apocalyptic vision John saw the pattern of heaven as a great spiritual idea coming down from heaven and abiding among men. To a Platonist there was no difficulty here. Heaven as a spiritual idea came from the eternal heaven wherein is the throne of God, and yet the eternal heaven remains as secure and real as ever. This pattern of heaven which came down to this world is the spiritual reality that we call the church. It lives among men as the passionate love and the inspiring thought of God. The man who enters it is already in heaven, not in his fleshly body, but in spiritual reality. Death is not the crisis for this man; for him the crisis is the baptism of the Holy Spirit, which fully assimilates him to the perfect will of God.

For the New Testament believer, therefore, the startling crisis of life is not stepping into eternity, but rather stepping into the fullness of the blessing of the gospel of Christ. From that moment he is already in heaven in spirit. Paul clarifies the matter when he writes, "for our conversation is in heaven"

(Phil. 3:20). Here the word "conversation" means citizenship, and Moffatt's translation is: "We are a colony of heaven," and that is the meaning of the passage. The Philippians understood this well because they were a colony of Rome. They were Romans with full rights of citizenship. There was no distinction between them and the other citizens of Rome. They were simply a little Rome of their own, a colony of Roman citizens outside the city of Rome. In the same way, says Paul, all believers are a colony of heaven in this world of human life.

MARCHING TO CANAAN

These truths help to illuminate the symbolism of Canaan as set down in the third and fourth chapters of the Book of Hebrews. Probably the majority of Christians regard Canaan as a type of heaven. Almost all Wesleyan teachers regard it as a type of the completely consecrated life. The truths here expounded make it clear that it would be perfectly proper to regard Canaan as a type of both these experiences; for in the full light of the New Testament they are both one. The justified believer struggles like the Israelites, sometimes for forty years, in the wilderness of an incomplete Christian experience. At Jordan he crosses into Canaan. In the light of Scripture that is a crisis more exacting than natural death; for it marks the complete movement of the soul into the heavenly state of final deliverance, insofar as full redemption and enjoyment of divine grace are concerned. Canaan represents the fullness of the blessing of the gospel of Christ. It is heaven begun here on earth.

ENTERING THE HOLY OF HOLIES

The symbolism of the Tabernacle has perplexed Christians for generations. The Tabernacle proper had two compartments: the outside room, called the holy place; and a sacred, inner chamber, called the holy of holies. Around the whole Tabernacle ran a wall enclosing a court. This court represents the state of a convicted, penitent sinner. The altar typifies Christ with his eternal sacrifice for sin. The laver represents the experience of the washing of regeneration, after which one enters the holy place as a regenerated and justified saint. But what does the holy of holies represent? Most Christians who think about the matter at all suppose that it typifies heaven, and I believe that is true. However, it does not represent the eternal heaven alone, but also the heavenly state realized here and now in time, for the temple of God is among men. In other words, the holy of holies represents the experience of entire sanctification, in which the believer enjoys the fullness of the blessing of the gospel of Christ. Further proof of this is found in the fact that Christians are exhorted to enter this holiest place here and now.

"Having therefore, brethren, boldness to enter into the holiest by the blood of Jesus, by a new and living way, which he hath consecrated for us, through the veil, that is to say, his flesh; and having an high priest over the house of God; let us draw near with a true heart in full assurance of faith, having our hearts sprinkled from an evil conscience [by the experience of regeneration], and our bodies washed with pure water [in baptism]" (Heb. 10:19-21).

The people who are here exhorted are brethren, and these same people are told to hold fast their profession (vs. 23). All the context proves conclusively that Christians are the ones addressed, and yet these Christians are exhorted to go on and enter the holy of holies by faith. This one passage alone would be convincing to any thoughtful person free of all dogmatic bias. To the same effect is the notable passage in which Christians are exhorted to leave the elementary principles of Christianity and go on to perfection (Heb. 6:1). An argument has been made here that this is only rhetoric. Christians, we are told, are urged to talk about something else. It is amazing that serious-minded men could use the Scriptures so lightly. If Christians are to go on talking about perfection, there is only one reason why they should do so, and that is because there is for them a duty of pressing into the experience of perfection so beautifully developed in the whole Book of Hebrews. No serious-minded Christian can degrade the noble march to perfection in the Book of Hebrews into a cheap exercise in rhetoric.

IV.
THE SECOND CRISIS AS CLEANSING

First of all, the second crisis is the moment of cleansing from the remains of inbred sin. This is what it has always meant in Wesleyan theology and I believe this is its meaning in the New Testament.

The New Testament clearly teaches that justified believers are still burdened with remains of the carnal mind until they are cleansed therefrom by the baptism of the Holy Spirit in the experience of entire sanctification. This proposition will be developed here in two phases: (1) to show the historical place of this doctrine in Protestant religious faiths; (2) to show its scriptural validity.

The doctrine of the remains of inbred sin in believers is fundamental to the teaching of entire sanctification as a second work of grace; for if believers are fully cleansed from inbred sin in regeneration there is no place for a second work of grace, and all any Christian need do is simply to grow in grace until he finishes his life and passes on to glory.

The modern holiness movement took its rise most directly from the teachings of John Wesley, who believed that justified believers still have the remains of inbred sin and that they may be cleansed from these remains in a second experience of the grace of God called entire sanctification. John Wesley wrote:

> QUESTION: When may a person judge himself to have attained this?
>
> ANSWER: When, after having been convinced of inbred sin, by a far deeper and clearer conviction than that which he experienced before justification, and after having experienced a gradual mortification of it, he experiences a total death to sin, and an entire renewal in the love and image of God, so as to "rejoice evermore," to "pray without ceasing," and in everything to give thanks.[1]

Scholars need no proof that to Wesley entire sanctification meant principally the destruction of the remains of inbred sin in the heart of the justified believer, but those who feel doubtful may satisfy their minds by the numerous passages on the subject in his writings, of which an example has been given.

1. John Wesley, *Plain Account of Christian Perfection*, p. 50.

In this connection it is interesting to ascertain the evidences which led Wesley to this conclusion. To many Christians of our day, living in a world infected by liberalism and modernism, the idea of a sinful, depraved human nature existing even in the unsaved seems improbable, perhaps. To the men of Wesley's time, however, it was, in conformity with scriptural teaching, regarded as perfectly reasonable. But there was a further reason for his belief. Wesley was a priest of the Church of England, sworn to uphold its *Thirty-Nine Articles of Faith.* One of these Articles reads in part as follows:

> Original sin standeth not in the following of Adam... but it is the fault and corruption of the nature of every man, that naturally is engendered of the offspring of Adam; whereby man is very far gone from original righteousness, and is of his own nature inclined to evil, so that the flesh lusteth always contrary to the spirit; and therefore in every person born into this world, it deserveth God's wrath and damnation. *And this infection of nature doth remain, yea in them that are regenerated;* whereby the lust of the flesh...is not subject to the Law of God.[2]

While it is true that many times ministers vow to support creeds which they do not believe, it is certain that this was not the case with Wesley. He believed that *this infection of nature remains in those that are regenerated.* We may add that this article still stands in the law of the Church of England

2. *The Thirty-Nine Articles of the Church of England* (1562), Art. IX.

and its sister communion, the Protestant Episcopal Church in the United States.

The Church of England was not alone in holding this view, however. Luther's *Small Catechism* says regarding baptism: "It signifies that *the old Adam in us* [baptized Christians] is to be drowned by daily sorrow and repentance." This doctrine is made a part of the creed of Lutheranism in the *Formula of Concord* (1576), which speaks of the merely formal obedience of the worldly, and adds: "*As also the regenerate do, so far as they are yet carnal.*"[3]

The *French Confession of Faith* (1559) says concerning original sin: "We believe, also, that this evil is truly sin, sufficient for the condemnation of the whole human race...*even after baptism it is still of the nature of sin*, but the condemnation of it is abolished for the children of God, out of his mere free grace and love."[4]

The Synod of Dort, representative of the Reformed Church of Holland, decreed in 1619, "Whom God calls, according to his purpose, to the communion of his Son our Lord Jesus Christ, and regenerates by the Holy Spirit, he delivers also from the dominion and slavery of sin in this life; *though not altogether from the body of sin.*"[5]

The *Westminster Confession of Faith* (1647), the historic confession of English-speaking Presbyterianism, said, "*This corruption of nature*, during this life, *doth remain in those that are regenerated.*"[6] On sanctification, the *Confession* says: "This

3. *The Formula of Concord* (1576), Art. VI.
4. *The French Confession of Faith* (1559), Art. XI.
5. *The Canons of the Synod of Dort,* Fifth Head of Doctrine, Art. I.
6. *The Westminster Confession of Faith* (1647), chap.6, sec. 5.

sanctification is throughout in the whole man, yet *imperfect in this life; there abideth still some remnants of corruption* in every part, *whence ariseth a continual and irreconcilable war,* the flesh lusting against the spirit, and the spirit against the flesh."[7]

These references have not been given to prove that the doctrine of inbred sin is scriptural, but merely to clarify the point that it is a universal doctrine of orthodox Protestantism. Here we have traced the very words of Lutheran, Reformed, Presbyterian, and Church of England creeds—each distinctly and separately expressing in plain language the belief that there are remains of carnality left in the regenerated.

And even the Roman Catholic Church, although it condemns the language of the Protestant creeds regarding original sin in believers, does teach the principle in effect, as may be seen by the following language of the Council of Trent:

> This holy Synod confesses and is sensible, that *in the baptized there remains concupiscence, or an incentive* (to sin); which, whereas it is left for our exercise, cannot injure those who consent not, but resist manfully by the grace of Jesus Christ.... This concupiscence, which *the Apostle sometimes calls sin* [here the reference is to Romans 6:12 and 7:8], the holy Synod declares that the Catholic church has never understood it to be called sin, as being truly and properly sin in those born again, but because *it is of sin, and inclines to sin.*[8]

7. Ibid., chap. 13, sec. 2. (Italics are the author's.).
8. The Council of Trent, decree concerning original sin. (Italics are the author's.).

We feel inclined to agree with the Council in a certain hesitation to call this nature "sin" for fear of misapprehension. In the same decree the Council says: "In those who are born again there is nothing that God hates." This is, however, a matter of terminology; for the Council admits that even *Paul himself called this element in believers by the name of sin.* And it is sin in the sense that it is prone to rebel against God.

Thus it has been proved by incontestable testimony that both the Roman Catholic Church and all the great churches of Protestantism have taught officially in their fundamental creeds that there is a nature of sin remaining in the regenerated. As has been before conceded, this does not prove the doctrine to be scriptural, but it does lay a burden of proof upon the objector. Surely there must be some reason why every great creed of the Western Christian world has definitely taught the continuing existence of the remains of carnality in the regenerated. What makes all Western Christendom hold this view? Catholic, Lutheran, Reformed, Presbyterian, and Church of England theologians—men as far apart as the poles in other phases of religious thinking—have agreed upon this principle. John Wesley simply went a step further when he said that although there is such a thing as carnality in believers, it is possible for them to find deliverance from that carnality in this life.

CARNALITY IN BELIEVERS

We know well enough how this historic faith of the church will be scoffed at and ridiculed by modernists and liberals. They will say that this belief is a product of the superstition and ignorance of the Dark Ages. When we hear such a reply we ought to remember that this belief was held by the heroic and martyrlike churches of the Sixteenth Century Reformation, as well as by the *older church.* Moreover, we might as well say that the doctrine of inbred sin in believers has been so completely woven into the very heart and fabric of the church's thought and life that it has been impossible to get rid of it, even though other doctrines might be discarded. The fact is that many, if not most, of those who scoff so loudly at the doctrine of sin in believers, actually do not believe in any doctrine of an inherited nature of sin, and they reject this doctrine of hereditary sinfulness because they are infected with modernism and naturalism to a point where they deride this historic doctrine of the church and of the Scriptures. It stands to reason that the doctrine which maintains the existence of inbred sin in believers must rest upon the general doctrine of original sin in all mankind; and this is the doctrine so completely taught in the Scriptures that no one can reject it without proclaiming himself a modernist, lacking reverence for the Word of God.

Since it is not of primary importance for unsaved people to understand the doctrine of sin in believers, it is not imperative that that truth should be revealed to them. Consequently, we find that it lies partly hidden in the Scriptures, to be discovered only by the pious thought of earnest seekers for the truth. Many intimations of this truth exist for those who are willing to see them in the Scriptures.

The Apostle Paul points out in Romans 7:5-24 the struggle of an awakened sinner striving to justify himself by the works of the law. This passage is cited to show the way this law of sin works in the hearts of earnest men who are awakened and have begun to seek God, although this does not describe the condition of a converted man. The whole question is, Does this conflict continue in any measure after the experience of regeneration? It is fundamental to the doctrine of entire sanctification to answer that it does; for if this is not true, then the whole doctrine of entire sanctification is nothing less than a delusion. In I Corinthians 3:1-4 the Apostle teaches plainly, for those who are willing to believe, that the babes in Christ are still afflicted with the mind of carnality: "And I, brethren, could not speak unto you as unto spiritual, but as unto carnal, even as unto babes in Christ.... For ye are yet carnal: for whereas there is among you envying, and strife, and divisions, are ye not carnal, and walk as men?" It would not do to say that this carnality simply refers to normal human nature. Prof. W. H. Howard says that the Greek term here translated "carnal" "is more distinctly ethical, 'having the characteristics of flesh,' 'carnally minded.'"[9] "It is a moral perversion."[10]

The Epistle to the Hebrews likewise addresses babes in Christ who are "become such as have need of milk, and not of strong meat" (5:12). The same writer warns "lest any root of bitterness springing up trouble you and thereby many be defiled" (12:15). This "root of bitterness" is the carnal nature. But the Apostle is very plain in writing to the Galatian church. Here he describes the conflicts in the heart of unsanctified

9. Prof. W. H. Howard, *The Abingdon Commentary*, p. 1175.

10. George Barker Stevens, *The Theology of the New Testament*, p. 345.

believers as follows: "The flesh lusteth against the Spirit, and the Spirit against the flesh: and these are contrary the one to the other: so that ye cannot [may not] do the things that ye would. But if ye be led of the Spirit, ye are not under the law" (Gal. 5:17-18). This is clearly a description of the conflict which goes on in the heart of regenerated men before they are entirely sanctified.

Regeneration is an experience in which the soul is forgiven and cleansed from all past sins. Likewise it is cleansed from the acquired depravity of a sinful life, and the power of the law of sin is broken in the heart. Nevertheless, this inherited depravity, which was in the heart of the infant, continues to abide in the heart of the believer until he receives the baptism of the Holy Ghost and of power, which fully purifies the heart from the last remains of the inherited, sinful nature, as Peter reported to the church at Jerusalem concerning the occasion of the baptism of the Holy Ghost upon the household of Cornelius. God, he explained, had sanctified the Gentile believers just as he had blessed the Jewish believers on the Day of Pentecost. "And put no difference between us and them, purifying their hearts by faith" (Acts 15:9). In the First Epistle of John there is a blessed promise to the obedient believers: "If we walk in the light, as he is in the light, we have fellowship one with another, and the blood of Jesus Christ his Son cleanseth us from all sin" (1:7).

Once a man discerns this fundamental truth of holiness, he can see a vast array of scriptures contributing confirmatory evidence to this view of truth.

Before a Christian proudly rejects this light he ought to remember that for many generations *this truth* has been the avenue of countless blessings for those who accepted and acted upon it. It has been the continual inspiration for an agelong revival; it is the reason of the existence of the holiness movement. In *this light* our fathers and grandfathers and the earnest and heroic pioneers of the holiness movement labored with sacrificial diligence and ascended triumphantly to their glorious rest in heaven.

Let us now proceed to a more detailed study of the nature of this inbred sin from which the believer is delivered in entire sanctification.

V.
SIN AS EVIL DISPOSITION

Four hundred years before Christ, Plato, the greatest of Greek philosophers, dreamed of an ideal state of human happiness. There people would live in temperance and simplicity. This is the way he imagined them:

> And when they are housed, they will work, in summer, commonly, stripped and barefoot, but in winter substantially clothed and shod. They will feed on barley meal and flour of wheat, baking and kneading them, making noble cakes and loaves; these they will serve up on a mat of reeds or on clean leaves, themselves reclining the while upon beds strewn with yew or myrtle. And they and their children will feast…wearing garlands on their heads, and hymning the praises of the

gods, in happy converse with one another....But, said Glaucon, interposing, you have not given them a relish for their meal.

True, I replied, I had forgotten; of course they must have a relish—salt, and olives, and cheese, and they will boil roots and herbs such as country people prepare; for a dessert we shall give them figs, and peas, and beans; and they will roast myrtle-berries and acorns at the fire....And with such a diet they may be expected to live in peace and health to a good old age, and bequeath a similar life to their children after them.

Yes, Socrates, he said, and if you were providing for a city of pigs, how else would you feed the beasts?

But what would you have, Glaucon? I replied.

Why, he said, you should give them the ordinary conveniences of life. People who are to be comfortable are accustomed to lie on sofas, and dine off tables, and they should have sauces and sweets in the modern style.

Yes, I said, now I understand: the question which you would have me consider is, not only how a State, but how a luxurious State is created; and possibly there is no harm in this, for in such a State we shall be more likely to see how justice and injustice originate. In my opinion the true and healthy constitution of the State is the one which I have described. But if you wish also to see a State at fever-heat, I have no objection. For I suspect that many will not be satisfied with the simpler way of life. They will be for adding sofas, and tables, and other furniture; also dainties, and perfumes, and

> incense, and courtesans, and cakes, all these not of one sort only, but in every variety; we must go beyond the necessaries of which I was at first speaking, such as houses, and clothes, and shoes: the arts of the painter and the embroiderer will have to be set in motion, and gold and ivory and all sorts of materials must be procured.
>
> True, he said.
>
> Then we must enlarge our borders; for the original healthy State is no longer sufficient. Now will the city have to fill and swell with a multitude of callings which are not required by any natural want; such as the whole tribe of hunters and actors, of whom one large class have to do with forms and colors; another will be the votaries of music—poets and their attendant train of rhapsodists, players, dancers, contractors; also makers of divers kinds of articles, including women's dresses. And we shall want more servants. Will not tutors be also in request, and nurses wet and dry, tirewomen and barbers, as well as confectioners and cooks; and swineherds, too, who were not needed and therefore had no place in the former edition of our State, but are needed now? They must not be forgotten: and there will be animals of many other kinds, if people eat them.[1]

Then Plato goes on to show how the natural passions and desires of men will multiply and grow. The country will become too small and then the neighbors' lands must be an-

1. *The Works of Plato,* translated by B. Jowett, pp. 65-67.

nexed, causing war. Thus one by one, Plato shows how men's desires grow up, and by their feverish demands for more than justice and temperance will admit, they tend constantly to cancel the plans of idealism. The evil passions and the sinful desires of men's hearts turn the dream of earthly Utopias into a nightmare of corrupt and vicious civilization, anarchy, and war.

We have not cited Plato's views because we agree with them in detail, by any means, but because they furnish an illustration of the fact that the inborn perversity of human nature has been an insoluble problem for those who have dreamed dreams of human welfare for the last 2,400 years.

Present-day idealistic dreamers base their plans for a bright future upon the present achievement and the promised development of science. It is true that science does point the way by which a race of good, just, and unselfish men could create an earthly paradise, but, unfortunately, science is not able to show how evil men can create such a desirable world; for when evil men obtain the secrets of power that will level the mountains and make the desert to bloom they use that power to seek to enslave their neighbors, and instead of leveling the mountains they level the fairest cities, and instead of making the desert bloom they destroy the culture and arts and the most precious blossoms of the civilization of mankind which have developed through a thousand years.

We sympathize with all the dreams of a better world. We long for that land of abundant comfort and beauty which science could provide, but we believe we are justified in directing attention to, and spending thought upon, the problem of changing men so that their hearts will be prepared to work together in building a world of peace and justice.

This approach makes it necessary for us to study the nature of man's singular perversities. What is there about him that makes him fiercer than any living animal? Why does he tend to change love into lust, to cast himself down from honor to infamy, to substitute rapacity for justice? Why does he tend to pervert government to despotism and to desecrate high office by the foulest of graft and corruption? Why does he seek to divert the wealth of a state, which would make all of its citizens prosperous, to a demonic effort to enslave neighboring states and peoples? Why does man degrade and defile every high and beautiful instinct of human nature? Why does he defile his own family life with tobacco, liquor, profanity, hatred, jealousy, and marital infidelity? Why does he profane the church with hypocrisy and prostitute its holiest offices to greed? Why does he make the State an instrument of torture for millions of his fellows?

Why has man always acted so perversely? What hope have we that he will ever cease this manner of life? We believe that the historic Christian church has always had the answers to these questions. Some of its teachers may have on occasion gone to extremes in expounding the Christian doctrine of depravity, but in the heart of that doctrine there lies a truth so sound and incontrovertible that it deserves the careful study of people of our times.

INDWELLING SIN

Just as there is opposition to the Christian doctrine of individual and personal guilt and sin, so there is also even wider opposition to the accompanying Christian doctrine of sin as inherited depravity, or race sin. Bear in mind that the term sin as used here in such expressions as "inherent sin" is used accommodatively to describe this corrupt and depraved nature as sin, because it comes originally from the act of sin in the beginning of the race and because it is characterized by an active tendency to sin. Paul used it in this connection and so did the Christian teachers of the ages.

It is a common observation of mankind that acts of sin tend to become habit, or disposition to sin, and this habit tends to form a certain, definite sinful character. This tendency toward sin, or personal depravity, is such a common experience of mankind that it needs no argument to prove it. The question now before us is whether such a tendency toward sin is capable of being transmitted by heredity. Is there such a thing as "race sin" or "inbred sin"? Here again we have the testimony of all the ages expressing the common belief of mankind that human nature has in it some hereditary element of depravity which tends to propagate itself anew in every social environment which man can devise.

Plato wrote: "But the point which I desire to note is that in all of us, even in good men, there is a lawless wild-beast nature, which peers out in sleep."

Many other citations from famous authors could be given. Even Kant (1804)—whom the electrical genius Steinmetz pronounced the greatest metaphysician who ever lived—was a believer in the doctrine of original sin, which he called "the radical evil" of human nature. Dr. C. E. M. Joad, of the University of London, formerly an atheist, in his book *God and Evil* says: "Evil is not merely a by-product of unfavorable circumstances. It is so widespread, so deep-seated that one can only conclude that what the religions have always taught is true and that evil is endemic in the heart of man."

Perhaps the modern psychologists have given the strongest scientific testimony to the correctness of the traditional doctrine of original depravity. Sigmund Freud and other profound researchers in this field have, as they believe, uncovered a very nest of unclean and evil beasts in the subconscious mind of human nature, and it is a most fascinating study to follow them in tracing an evil tendency from the cellar of the human soul disguising itself as something good and beautiful in order to thrust its evil face into the daylight of the conscious mind.

This psychology has passed through the fires of criticism to a point which gives assurance that its major results will endure as permanent principles of a scientific estimate of human nature. Man is undoubtedly corrupt, judged from any elevated moral standpoint. His depravity, like breaches in the stone wall of an ancient castle, runs clear down to the foundations of his life.

A study of depravity is one of the most practical importance. An architect seeking to build a large structure must know the strength of his material; and if he learns that all of his steel beams are fractured in one way or another and he cannot get other material in their place, but must use them, then he must redesign the height, size, and form of his structure. Likewise all politicians, statesmen, social reformers, philanthropists, and lovers of mankind would do well to understand the strength of human nature as revealed by history, science, psychology, and the study of the Holy Scripture.

THE CHANGE MADE BY ADAM'S FALL

This teaching on depravity is best understood by a survey of the conditions of Adam's probation, his tragic fall, and the dismal heritage which he left to mankind. The Bible says that "God hath made man upright; but they have sought out many inventions" (Eccles. 7:29). Paul says that "by one man sin entered into the world" (Rom. 5:12).

Everything in that early world, including man, was good (Gen. 1:31). Man lived in a world that knew no sin and he enjoyed dominion over all the lower animals and over all nature (Gen. 1:28). Moreover he enjoyed fellowship and communion with God.

The old-time theologians exalted the intellectual ability of Adam. He was, they said, of a giant mind, more able and mighty than any of his fallen descendants. The later theologians have scoffed at these views, regarding Adam as having been very low indeed in the scale of mental development. Adam's intelligence rating must have been a very high and worthy one, living as he did in perfect innocence and holiness and in the very fullness of the powers with which God created him. Moreover, there is no proof that he did not spend considerable time in this state.

The reason his state was so excellent was because he was made in the image and likeness of God: "And God said, Let us make man in our image, after our likeness....So God created man in his own image, in the image of God created he him; male and female created he them" (Gen. 1:26-27).

Of what did this image consist: "And have put on the new man, which is renewed in knowledge after the image of him that created him" (Col. 3:10).

Here the distinctive character of this image is the *power to know.* And surely in it does man far transcend the beasts. Again we read, "And that ye put on the new man, which after God is created in righteousness and TRUE HOLINESS" (Eph. 4:24).

In these two texts we have the double character of the divine image. It was a reflection in finite form of the infinite character of God. In the first text the image is intellectual knowledge, as of a free and conscious spirit; and in the second text we see the moral nature of God as righteousness and true holiness. These two phases of the divine image are sometimes called the natural and moral image of God. The moral image of God was one that man could and did lose, namely, righteousness and true holiness.

The natural image of God, the capacity for knowledge, by which man became a living soul and attained to human personality, was not destroyed; and it is that image, together with some faint traces of the moral character of God, which makes man capable of salvation. The natural image of God, even to this day, is man's possibility of surmounting his prejudices and passions and rising to a thought which in its broken and finite way is like the majestic thought of God. "I am thinking God's thoughts after Him," declared Kepler ecstatically as he worked out the motion of the planets by the methods of science.

Possessing the image of God, Adam had dominion over the animals, over nature, and over his own natural body so that his emotions, appetite, and instincts were all free from the disease of sin. He also had access to the tree of life. Undoubtedly Adam's body was naturally mortal to some extent, like that of the lower animals. Nevertheless, he lived in the spiritual atmosphere of eternity in such fellowship with God that surely his body would eventually have taken on immortality and enjoyed glorification just as the bodies of the saints will enjoy it at the resurrection. The tree of life was a symbol of this divine medicine of immortality.

This is the sense in which death came upon all men. As a result of sin, man was barred from access to the means of physical immortality. And this consequence of sin was made so sharp that the body was not able to partake of the full benefit of the atonement in its rescue from physical death until it had fulfilled its appointment to death. Paul said he was waiting for "the adoption, to wit, the redemption of the body," in the glory of the resurrection (Rom. 8:23).

Some have regarded the prohibition against eating the fruit of the tree of knowledge as being a trivial ordinance. It is evident that this prohibition in itself did not fully describe the central law of holiness and mutual love between God and man. It was simply a positive command, reasonable in its purpose, easy to fulfill, and yet furnishing man a very mild and simple test at the beginning of his probation.

The simplicity of the provision may be regarded as being well adapted to the kindergarten stage of man's moral and spiritual education. Undoubtedly, if he had passed that test successfully he would have ascended step by step to loftier and more perilous heights in which, had he proved faithful, he would have advanced to nobler and more complex conflicts out of which, if faithful, he would have emerged a moral and spiritual giant—a worthy son of God. And there is no doubt that he would have transmitted a fine character to his children.

That the natural image of God, meaning the spiritual nature of human personality, cannot be destroyed is the verdict of Scripture: "Whoso sheddeth man's blood, by man shall his blood be shed: FOR IN THE IMAGE OF GOD MADE HE MAN" (Gen. 9:6). In other words, even the fallen men who live after Adam retain the natural image of God and, consequently, a sacredness inheres in their personality. "Therewith bless we God, even the Father; and therewith curse we men, which are made AFTER THE SIMILITUDE OF GOD" (James 3:9). It is the possession of this natural image of God which makes all doctrines of annihilation false and proves the immortality of the human spirit.

THE EFFECT OF THE FALL

When Adam received the prohibition against eating the fruit of the tree of knowledge, he was warned that "in the day that thou eatest thereof thou shalt surely die." This death was primarily a death of separation from God. In other words, the loss of the moral image of God befell Adam in the day that he ate the forbidden fruit.

It is also evident that the sentence included physical death. But Adam continued to live hundreds of years after that time, therefore we believe that immediate death was suspended on account of the universal grace coming to all men through the atonement of Christ, which instituted for Adam and for mankind another probation. The first probation was for Adam as the head of the natural human race. The second probation was under the second Adam, Christ.

However, part of the consequences of Adam's sin followed swiftly and tragically. He was excluded from the Garden of Eden and introduced into the toil and sorrow of the lower region of life. If, as we believe, the Scripture teaches the moral image of God was in righteousness and true holiness, then we must see that possession of that image implies a distinct desire and tendency to love and serve God. Just as it is natural for fish to swim in the sea, for birds to fly through the air, and for the wild fowl to move southward in the autumn, so it is an instinct of man's soul to reach out toward God in loving fellowship and humble obedience.

The loss of the image of God planted an opposite tendency in man's soul, and Adam transmitted that tendency to all mankind. After he lost the image of God, "Adam begat a son in his own likeness" (Gen. 5:3). That is, in the image of Adam, and not in the image of God.

THE TEACHING OF THE APOSTLE PAUL

That a sinful nature was inherited by all men from Adam is the plain teaching of the Apostle Paul. Remembering that the word sin is here used in an accommodative sense as describing a tendency toward sin, and that death for innocent infants is not a penalty but a consequence of the sin of Adam, we follow Paul's argument: "Death passed upon all men, for that all have sinned" (Rom. 5:12). It came even over them "that had not sinned after the similitude of Adam's transgression" (5:14).

Thus we see that when man sinned he lost something essential out of his nature; he lost the image of God in the sense of moral likeness to God. This deprivation made it impossible for him to live a good and righteous life, just as the loss of one leg makes it impossible for a man to walk. But this loss led also to depravation, just as the loss of teeth out of the jaw of a growing child makes the jawbone grow into an abnormal shape. When human nature lost the image of God and power to live holy it became depraved and bent into crooked and abnormal forms, contrary to the original intention of the Father.

This doctrine of inherited depravity does not contradict the justice of God and is not inconsistent with sound reasoning. Also, this inherited depravity does not in and of itself involve guilt. Infants are not guilty, but as they grow into adult life they invariably fall into sin through the depraved character of the nature which they inherit from Adam.

CONSEQUENCE AND PENALTY

Here it is necessary to show a distinction between consequence and penalty. Suppose a quarrelsome and contentious man should become involved in a brawl wherein he loses the use of one hand for life and for this brawl the judge sentences him to six months in jail. The sentence of the judge is the *penalty* for man's crime, but the lifelong disability of being a cripple is the *consequence* of his crime. The judge never appointed the *consequences* and cannot remove them. On account of his being a lifelong cripple the man's children may suffer the disadvantages of poverty, ignorance, and much misery. This also is not a *penalty* for them, but a *consequence* of their father's sin.

The Apostle Paul shows that in the same way death is the *consequence* of Adam's sin. It passed upon all men even though individuals, i.e., infants among them, had not sinned the same sin as Adam himself had committed. However, the consequence of sin becomes a penalty in the child who accepts the transgression and the guilt as his own by an active choice upon reaching the age of accountability. By so doing he likewise accepts the penalty of sin.

Here it could be said that it is not just that an innocent child should suffer death as a consequence, whereas a wicked man suffers death as a penalty; but the child knows nothing of the misery and pain and fear of death which comes as a penalty to the adult sinner.

Paul compares the first Adam with Christ, who is the second Adam. "If through the sins of one many be dead, much more the grace of God, and the gift by grace, which is by one man, Jesus Christ, hath abounded unto many. And not as it was by one that sinned, so is the gift: for the judgment was by one to condemnation, but the free gift is of many offenses unto justification" (Rom. 5:15-16).

As is pointed out in *The Meaning of Salvation* (p. 122f), the justification of infants is conditional, just as their guilt is conditional: if, when they grow up, they accept the guilt of Adam's sin by participating in it, they become guilty and are participants in the guilt of race sin. If, on the contrary, they accept the justification in Christ, they may also receive that justification by faith in his atoning death. "For as by one man's disobedience many were made sinners, so by the obedience of one shall many be made righteous" (Rom. 5:19).

"As in Adam all die, even so in Christ shall all be made alive" (I Cor. 15:22). "The first man Adam was made a living soul; the last Adam was made a quickening spirit" (I Cor. 15:45).

"The sting of death is sin" means that although death is a consequence of Adam's sin upon all men, it is without sting except for those who have the conscious guilt of sin.

THE BIBLE TEACHES THE DOCTRINE OF INBRED SIN

The Jews of Christ's time spoke truly when they told the blind man that he had been "altogether born in sins" (John 9:34), and it was Jesus who said "that which is born of the flesh is flesh" (John 3:6). Soon after man was expelled from the Garden of Eden "God saw that the wickedness of man was great in the earth, and that every imagination of the thoughts of his heart was only evil continually. And it repented the Lord that he had made man on the earth, and it grieved him at his heart" (Gen. 6:5-6).

This does not mean that God repented as men do, but that since man had changed his attitude toward God, God automatically must change his attitude toward man. After the flood "the Lord said in his heart...the imagination of man's heart is evil from his youth" (Gen. 8:21). David confessed: "I was shapen in iniquity; and in sin did my mother conceive me" (Ps. 51:5). Christ taught that evil thoughts and a whole long catalogue of sins proceed out of the heart (Matt. 15:19). "Ye then, BEING EVIL, know how to give gifts unto your children" (Matt. 7:11), said Christ. In other words, he took it for granted that they were evil in their hearts. Paul said that "we have borne the image of the earthy" (I Cor. 15:49), meaning that we inherited the image of Adam. Christ told the Jews of his time, "Ye are from beneath; I am from above; ye are of this world; I am not of this world" (John 8:23).

Christ was unique because of the fact that "in him is no sin" (I John 3:5). James calls this sinful nature lust: "Every man is tempted, when he is drawn away of his own lust, and enticed. Then when lust hath conceived, it bringeth forth sin; and sin, when it is finished, bringeth forth death" (Jas. 1:14-15).

But for Paul it is "the law of sin and death" (Rom. 8:2); "sin that dwelleth in me"; "the law of sin" (7:17, 23). He also says that "the carnal mind is enmity against God" (Rom. 8:7) and that the heathen Ephesians before their conversion were "BY NATURE the children of wrath" (Eph. 2:3). This does not mean that they were under the wrath of God as children; this is a Hebraism—"children of wrath" means *people under wrath.*

Full proof that this sinful disposition is in children before they reach the age of accountability is given by Paul in these words: "I was alive without the law once: but when the commandment came [that means when he became conscious of the commandment], SIN REVIVED, and I died" (Rom. 7:9). How could sin revive unless it was already in his heart in a latent form? This was the "SIN THAT DWELLETH IN ME" (Rom. 7:20), the "LAW IN MY MEMBERS, warring against the law of my mind, and bringing me into captivity to THE LAW OF SIN which is in my members" (Rom. 7:23). "O wretched man that I am! Who shall deliver me from the BODY OF THIS DEATH?" (Rom. 7:24).

The body of death is the carnal mind, *the inborn nature of sin.* This fallen man is without God and without hope in the world (Eph. 2:12).

Further proof of the sinful nature of all mankind is furnished by the sweeping statement of Paul in the quotation set down in the third chapter of Romans: "There is none righteous, no not one." And both Jews and Gentiles are all under sin, for, says John, "if we say we HAVE NO SIN, we deceive ourselves, and the truth is not in us." This undoubtedly refers to the *inbred nature of sin* and *the sinful tendency* which corrupts the lives of all mankind.

VI.
THE DOCTRINE OF INHERITED SIN

It is not uncommon to read in theological works some expression to the effect that the doctrine of original sin was unknown to the New Testament church and was never introduced until the days of Augustine. Such statements could not do very much harm, perhaps, if the readers understood the subject. The only way a scholar could make such a remark conscientiously is by giving a special definition to the doctrine of original sin. If by original sin he means a sinful state of the infant for which it stands guilty before God, the statement might have some meaning; but if we define original sin in the sense in which it is used in this book, namely, as an hereditary inclination of the heart to evil, but not as incurring guilt in infants, then the doctrine of original sin is very plainly taught throughout the Old Testament and in Judaism before the time of Christ and Paul. Regarding the teaching of the Old Testament, Dr. Gustav S. Oehler, of Tübingen University, writes as follows:

> ***The State of Sin***
>
> ***Sin as an Inclination. Transmission of Sin.***
>
> In consequence of the Fall, sin appears as a *state* of mankind—that is, as an *inclination* which rules man, and as a common sinful life which is transmitted partly in mankind in general, and partly in an especial degree in particular races, and so subjects these to the curse of guilt and judgment.
>
> 1. After once appearing by the free act of man, sin does not remain in this isolation. The *second* sin, that of self-excuse and palliation of the offense, follows immediately on the first, the sin of disobedience (Gen. 3:10). This is the deceit (Ps. 32:2), which, when sin has once entered, prevents the realization of earnest opposition thereto. As sin thus joins to sin, it becomes a *habitus*, and in this way a definite feature of the heart, or, as it is termed, a *yetzer lev*, imagination of the heart, an *inclination*, which gives a perverted tendency to man's will. Thus it is said before the flood (Gen. 6:5), "Every imagination [*yetzer*] of the thoughts of his heart is only evil continually;" and after it again (8:21): "The imagination [*yetzer*] of man's heart is evil from his youth. That this [*yetzer*] is not to be understood simply as a physical disposition, as is taught by Rabbinical theology, is shown by the more exact expression in 6:5

(compare I Chron. 28:9). Because this sinful inclination—this is the meaning of the variously explained passage Genesis 8:21—cleaves to man from his youth, the human race would lie under a continual sentence of destruction if God gave severe justice its course. The ground for sparing him is, according to the context of that passage, that man still seeks communion with God, as is shown by sacrifice. The natural striving of man against God's law—the stiffneckedness and hardness of heart so often spoken of in the Pentateuch—is based on this *sinful inclination.* Therefore, when Israel promises to keep the divine law, the divine voice complains (Deut. 5:28-29): "They have spoken right, but oh, that they had a heart to fear me and keep all my commands."

2. That this *sinful inclination is hereditary* [italics the author's] is indirectly contained in the passages cited, although it is not expressly said. It is also to be noticed, that Mosaism, although it derives the propagation of man's race from God's blessing, still regards all events and conditions which refer to birth and generation as requiring a purifying expiation; compare the law (Lev. 12:16) in which the thought lies that all these conditions are connected with the disturbance of sin. Hence Psalm 51:7 expresses the idea of the law: "Behold, I was born in iniquity, and in sin did my mother conceive me." Even if this passage spoke only of an iniquity and sin of the *parents,* according to the explanation which is now more common, it would still follow, from

> the fact that *the very origin of man is connected with sin* [italics mine], that even the newly-born child is not free from sin; as Job 14:4 expresses it, "How can a clean thing come from an unclean? Not one"—a thought which is certainly connected with the passage in the Psalms. But there is nothing to prevent iniquity and sin in the passages in the Psalms being referred, as is done by Hitzig, to the child itself as soon as conceived and born; according to which, the passage says directly that evil is ingrown in man from the first moment of his origin.[1] [Here I have transliterated part of the Hebrew quotations.]

JEWISH TEACHING IN THE APOSTOLIC AGE

The Jewish teachers of the time of Christ taught that man was created with two inclinations: an inclination *(yetzer)* toward good, and another inclination *(yetzer)* toward evil.[2] This evil *(yetzer)* worked in man from the beginning of time, but it was the thing which made infants inclined to sin. That the Jews of the first century taught the inheritance of this evil nature from Adam is plainly set forth in IV Ezra. This Jewish book is dated by scholars somewhere between AD 70 and 100, but it certainly reflects Jewish belief in the time of Christ; for that belief would scarcely change overnight. In it we read:

> And yet thou didst not take away from them *the evil heart,* that thy Law might bring forth fruit in them.

1. Gustav Friedrich Oehler, *Theology of the Old Testament,* pp. 161-162.
2. Alfred Edersheim, *The Life and Times of Jesus the Messiah,* p. 167.

> For the *first Adam, clothing himself with the evil heart,* transgressed and was overcome; and *likewise also all who were born of him.* Thus the infirmity became inveterate; the law indeed was in the heart of the people, but (in conjunction) with *the evil germ;* so what was good departed, and the evil remained.... The inhabitants of the City committed sin, in all things doing even as Adam and all his generations had done: for they also had clothed themselves with the evil heart....
>
> Who is there of those who have come (into the world) that has not sinned?...And now I see that the coming Age shall bring delight to few, but torment unto many. For the evil heart has grown up in us which has estranged us from God...and that not a few only, but well nigh all that have been created!...For though it was thou that sinned, the fall was not thine alone, but ours also who are thy descendants![3]

In the apocryphal book, The Wisdom of Sirach, written about 180 BC, we also have evidence of Jewish belief in inherited sin:

> O wicked thought! Why were you shaped
> To cover the earth with deceit?[4]

Here the base nature is the *yetzer-ha-ra,* or evil inclination, or tendency toward evil—"the imagination of man's heart" (Gen. 8:21).

3. *Apocrypha,* IV Ezra 3:21-28; 7:46-48, 118-119. (Italics are the author's.).
4. *Apocrypha,* The Wisdom of Sirach 37:3.

Inasmuch as the Jews of Christ's time believed in an inherited evil nature, one must think that the New Testament writers would have denied this doctrine if they had rejected it. On the contrary, that they write in the same vein themselves is proof that they taught some such doctrine.

HOW SHALL WE THINK OF INBRED SIN?

Among the pious young people of our times this has become a tantalizing question. Undoubtedly, here is a massive psychological fact worthy of the deepest study, and yet no scientific psychologist has ever dealt with it in terms of sin. This very fact will puzzle some students, although others will understand that physical science is by definition and by the very nature of its task precluded from transgressing into the fields of religion and theology. For this reason it must ignore some of the most colossal facts in human nature, such as the ever-present and enduring tendency to sin. As previously noted, modern depth psychologists, Freudians in particular, have at last taken notice of this outstanding quality of human nature which makes it so antisocial, but by the traditions of science even they are shut up to a nonreligious approach to the subject. They are bound to study it from a secular viewpoint if they are to give it any attention whatever.

But we, as Christian students and believers in the Word of God, are shut up to no such narrow method. In fact, we are bound to study this enormous abnormality in human nature from the standpoint of scriptural and Christian thought. Nevertheless, we find that the Lord Jesus translated the profound and hidden facts of the spiritual life into the simple forms of country life and work which he saw around him.

THE MEANING OF INSTINCT

In the language of our own times, just what is this "radical evil" of Immanuel Kant? this *yetzer-ha-ra* of the ancient Hebrew teacher, this "body of sin" of Paul? In order properly to study this question it is necessary first to glance at the meaning of instinct. Hitherto, we have hesitated to use the word instinct, as that term has been criticized by modern psychologists. However, all psychologists admit the facts of the nature of living things which correspond to the common word instincts. We may call these urges, appetites, unconscious patterns of behavior, or whatever we will. A recent edition of Webster's dictionary defines instinct as follows:

> A tendency to actions which lead to the attainment of some goal natural to the species; natural and unreasoning prompting to action; as, the web-building *instinct* of spiders. As distinguished from habit, *instinct* is not dependent on the individual's previous experience; as distinguished from emotion, it is a tendency to an external act affecting the environment; and, as distinguished from a reflex, it is more complex, more adaptable, and less stereotyped, and may involve a conscious impulse to activity.

Examples of instinctive action are young storks, which although they were hatched in northern latitudes and never saw any other, will on the approach of autumn wend their way to the south. Even a single stork that never saw any other stork in his life will do just that. This point is also illustrated by the way sparrows build their nest without any training. Such also is the behavior of bees in making their cells, and they will even make larger cells for young queen bees. Notice, too, the way in which a caterpillar will weave his shroud and prepare the way for the butterfly which he is to become later, although at present utterly unaware of that fact.

INSTINCTIVE HOLINESS

It seems to us that a modern philosopher, Henri Bergson, unintentionally gave a suggestion regarding the nature of inbred sin. Observing how nests of ants and hives of bees will patiently and sacrificingly work together for the good of the whole group, Bergson guessed that the original instincts of human nature were like that. It was, he thought, originally instinctive in humanity that without taking thought everyone should unconsciously and naturally do the thing, and follow the pattern of behavior, that would contribute most to the welfare of the whole of humanity. When the mind of man was lifted to the height of conscious intelligence, the bonds of instincts were weakened, and under the promptings of selfish desire man excused himself from working for the good of others and centered his attention and effort upon the attainment of his own selfish ends.

It is noticeable that man has very few complex patterns of instinct, such as those of ants, bees, beavers, and the like. His complex patterns of instinct have been broken up by the tremendous expansion of his intellect, which suggests new and varied patterns of conduct, capable of yielding him more abundant and specific satisfaction of his natural desires. This fact supports the suggestion previously made that it was in some such way as this that his original sound moral instinct was broken by the abuse of intelligence and the satisfaction of individual personal desires; also that even a wholly sanctified man, who has had his sound moral instincts reconstituted by the grace of God, will, because of his comparatively great intelligence, find a tension in deciding against personal selfish impulses in favor of his godly moral instincts—much greater than any tension a beaver would have in deciding to build a dam, or which a stork would have in deciding to fly south in the fall.

The exact measure of this tension could be almost scientifically stated as the difference between the intelligence of the man and the stork. In other words, intelligence and freedom furnish the grounds of man's first probation and the occasion of his first fall. While he lives in this world they will never cease to have the same meaning in his moral life.

No kind of instinct could ever be as strong in a highly intelligent being as it would be in an animal without the intelligence to suggest methods of doing things other than the instinctive methods. The lower animals do not have to balance instinct against impulse, as even a holy man must often do.

Some Christians may object to this picture because Bergson was an evolutionist, but if we remember that it is only a kind of parable, I think we can apply it to the Biblical representation of man's original nature and fall. The original state of man, according to the Bible, was sinless and gifted with the moral image of God. Was he not then as Bergson imagined him to have been, except that he had high intelligence and sound moral instincts at the very beginning? Nevertheless, Bergson comes near to the truth when he describes the Fall as being from original instinctive goodness and social co-operativeness, to the present anarchy of selfish individualistic desire; for the Bible teaches clearly that it was man's intelligence and capacity for choice that furnished the occasion for his fall.

When, according to the story, Adam broke that pattern, he shattered an instinct which we know as the moral image of God, an instinct which has never been put together again in human nature, except by a miracle of the grace of God.

One thing to remember in this figure of Bergson's is that being philosophical, it is nontheological; consequently, Bergson omitted the place of God in man's original sound moral instinct, but we do not need to omit that, and when we place that firmly in position we can see what possession of the moral image of God in Adam must have meant. It meant that Adam would instinctively do by preference and inward bent of desire those things which would contribute to the welfare of the whole human race whenever it came into existence and would express the love and devotion of his heart to God as Father and personal Friend.

CAN INSTINCT BE SINFUL?

Dr. Sangster has challenged the common doctrine that the instincts of a sinful man may be sinful instincts. He identifies the sinful instincts of humanity with the normal urges of human life, such as the hunger for food, sexual desire, self-respect, and the like. These, he thinks cannot be sinful in themselves. It is only when they are consciously yielded to sin that they may be said to be of the nature of sin.

In reply, it can be said that these impulses of human nature, which make life possible both in its beginning and in its continuance, were not essentially sinful in themselves at the beginning. This can be conceded, because we believe that Adam possessed these natural urges at the beginning of his existence. What we hold is that these urges have been infected and poisoned by the nature of sin, just as if a man should get arthritis in his hand, which would cause his hand to swell and be painful and deformed. Such a man would not want his hand cut off, but, in popular language, he would want "something taken out" of it, namely, the fever and the disease. That figure fairly well describes the infection of sin in the impulses of human nature.

Furthermore, there is a strange quality about instinct to which previous allusion has been made, namely, it combines many natural impulses into a distinct pattern of behavior that produces a result entirely unforeseen and not consciously planned. The original nature of man, as Bergson has suggested, was endowed with an instinct like that, directed toward moral and religious living. Adam's fall involved a breaking up of that instinctive pattern of moral and religious behavior. The *lack of that instinctive pattern*, together with the infection of man's impulses by self-regarding desires, lays the citadel of man's soul *open to sin* through every avenue of his being.

Broken fragments of the original instincts remain in the most evil and depraved heart which, when touched by the Spirit of God, awaken a hope of holiness and salvation in the most wicked soul. But the tendency toward sin does *not need any organized pattern; for in its essential nature sin is anarchy.* Holiness, however, represents a definite pattern of life that cannot successfully be followed in constant warfare against an inward tendency to sin. Moreover, consistent pursuit of the good life requires something like an instinctive organization of all man's powers to follow the ideal of holiness, not merely by will power, but by inward desire.

FIGURES OF DEPRAVITY

From the beginning of man's thought about the eternal, he has been baffled by all efforts to describe the invisible things of the spirit in the language of his earthly life. It has always been necessary to use figures of speech to say that this is like that. Despisers of religion have mocked this use of figurative language in all religious literature. In doing so they have scoffed at all the terminology of man's intelligent life, which lifts him above the beast; for not only the language of religion, but also the language of the intellect, is based upon figures of speech. Prof. W. S. Jevons, in his book on logic, has described this process as follows:

METAPHORICAL EXTENSION OF MEANING

In addition to the effects of generalization and specialization, vast additions and changes are made in language by the process of metaphorical extension of the meaning of words.

This change may be said no doubt, to consist in generalization since there must always be a resemblance between the new and old applications of the term. But the resemblance is often one of a most distant and obscure kind, such as we should call analogy rather than identity. All words used metaphorically, or as similitudes, are cases of this process of extension. The name metaphor is derived from the Greek words, "meta," over, and "pherein," to carry; and expresses apparently the transference of a word from its ordinary to a peculiar purpose. Thus the old similitude of a ruler to the pilot of a vessel gives rise to many metaphors, as in speaking of the prime minister being at the *helm* of the state. The word *governor,* and all its derivatives, is, in fact, one result of this metaphor, being merely a corrupt form of *gubernator, steersman.*

"The words *compass, polestar, ensign, anchor,* and many others connected with navigation, are constantly used in a metaphorical manner. From the use of horses and hunting we derive another series of metaphors; as, in taking the *reins* of government, *overturning* the government, *taking the bit between the teeth,* the government *whip, being heavily weighted,* etc. No doubt it might be shown that every other important occupation of life has furnished its corresponding stock of metaphors.

ORIGIN OF THE MENTAL VOCABULARY

This process, besides going on consciously at the present day, must have acted throughout the history of language, and we owe to it almost all, or probably all, the words expressive of refined mental or spiritual ideas. The very word *spirit,* now the most refined and immaterial of ideas, is but the Latin *spiritus,* a gentle breeze or breathing; and inspiration, *esprit,* or *wit,* and many other words, are due to this metaphor. It is truly curious, however, that almost all the words in different languages denoting mind or soul imply the same analogy to breath. Thus soul is from the Gothic root denoting a strong wind or storm; the Latin words *animus* and *anima* are supposed to be connected with the Greek *anemos* wind; psychic is certainly derived from *psucho* to blow; *pneuma,* air or breath, is used in the New Testament for Spiritual Being, and our word *ghost* has a similar origin.

Almost all the terms employed in mental philosophy or metaphysics, to denote actions or phenomena of mind, are ultimately derived from metaphors. Apprehension is the putting forward of the hand to take anything; comprehension is the taking of things together in a handful; extension is the spreading out; intention, the bending to; explication, the unfolding; application, the folding to; conception, the taking up together; relation, the carrying back; experience is the thoroughly going through a thing; difference is the carrying apart; deliberation, the weighing out; interruption, the breaking between; proposition, the placing before; intuition, the seeing into; and the list might be almost indefinitely extended. Our English name for reason, the understanding, obviously contains some physical metaphor which has not been fully explained; with the Latin intellect there is also a metaphor.

Every sense gives rise to words of refined meaning; sapience, taste, insipidity, gout are derived from the sense of taste; sagacity, from the dog's extraordinary power of smell; but as the sense of sight is by far the most acute and intellectual, it gives rise to the larger part of language; clearness, lucidity, obscurity, haziness, perspicuity, and innumerable other expressions, are derived from this sense.

These scientific facts give us an insight into the meaning and positive necessity of figurative language and parables in all attempts to describe mental and spiritual things.

INBRED SIN AS A ROOT

In the past a great deal of ridicule has been poured upon the efforts of the pioneers to describe the carnal nature as the root of the tree whose branches become developed habits of sin and whose evil fruit is likened to transgression and the results of a sinful life. In a previous passage I have attempted to give a modern estimate of the meaning of inbred sin. Nevertheless, long contemplation of the subject fails to shake my opinion that the figure of a tree, whose roots are carnality and whose fruits are transgression, is still a valid parable of this evil element in the human life.

It is true that Dr. W. E. Sangster, in his recent book, *The Path to Perfection,* mildly censures the idea of eradicating sin, or of thinking of sin as "a thing." He condemns the idea that sin can exist in the heart like a cancer or a rotten tooth.

However, we are only using figurative language when we speak of the "root of bitterness" (Heb. 12:15). If we were debating with physical scientists, who think of "things" as being physical substance like rocks, stones, trees, etc., we might have as great a debate over whether the soul itself is a "thing" as whether the nature of sin is a "thing." Viewed from the physical standpoint, a transgression that pollutes human nature is not a "thing," but a relationship to God. That, of course, is true. Nevertheless, throughout the Bible writers describe this condition as filth and pollution, from which we are washed by the blood of Christ.

Just what shall we call that instinctive pattern of evil laid down in the very constitution of human nature, corrupting the life of all human society everywhere. It is *a tendency toward sin,* just as there is a *tendency* in a straightened wire spring to return to its former condition. Strictly speaking we know that this tendency in the spring to coil is not a *thing* in the spring. Nevertheless, it is a *pattern* in the spring, and it represents a certain conformation of the materials of the spring. Those materials lack the inner pattern of arrangement that makes them tend to lie straight. They possess a bent which makes them curve.

INBRED SIN AND DIVINE JUSTICE

Perhaps the weightiest objection in popular belief to the doctrine of inbred sin is that it would be unjust for God to allow children to be born into the world handicapped by an inherited nature of sin at the moment when they are as innocent as lambs. The answer to this is that in the Arminian view of inbred sin it is first of all *the lack of something:* it is the lack of the image of God, and inherited sin is the *inheritance of the poverty of Adam* and the poverty of the race. A man with ten million dollars may through poor management lose it all and his child will *inherit his poverty.* In logical language we might say that the child did not inherit anything, but to the child his inheritance will seem a very positive evil. This question as to whether sin is *something*, like a cancer, or whether it is *nothing*, like blindness, being, as it is, *the absence of something*, has puzzled theologians for ages. Undoubtedly it is easier to understand the doctrine of inbred sin as being a reasonable consequence of Adam's transgression if we think of it as the *loss of something*—just as *blindness* is not the addition of something, but the *loss of something*, i. e., the loss of sight. Inbred sin is the *loss of the image of God.* Experience shows us that such poverty and such negative consequences of a parent's sin do fall upon children all over the world and in all times; and it is a waste of words to say that it is not just, for *it is obviously a part of the nature of the universe.*

We do not mean there is nothing positive in the nature of inbred sin. We regard the *positive evil of inbred sin* to be *corruption* arising from a lack of the image of God. We might illustrate it in this way: A person lacks lime in his bones. On account of this lack of lime the weight of his body makes his leg bones bend until they are badly deformed. The deformity illustrates the corruption of man's nature arising from the defect due to the lack of the image of God. Blindness is certainly a positive evil, and yet it arises from the lack of sight. That usually comes from a defect in the eye itself.

Another objection is: How can there be any distinction between regeneration and entire sanctification? The answer is that in regeneration all the sins of the individual are forgiven, the corruption of his nature arising from his own misbehavior is removed, but the inherited depravity, or bent of his nature, is not removed. There is still a lack of the perfect image of God. This lack is compensated in the heart of the Christian by the supernatural grace of God, but it is not completely made up until he is entirely sanctified and his heart is purified by faith.

Another objection is of a self-contradictory nature. People who do not believe in inbred sin and those who believe it is all removed in conversion or by baptism or by confirmation, nevertheless pour their ridicule on those who believe it is removed by faith through the sanctifying baptism of the Holy Ghost and the atoning work of Christ. Infidels, atheists, and liberal Christians have no right to ridicule this cleansing, because they all teach that people are not born with a sinful nature; and if that is true, then our claim to be free from that nature is—or ought to be—considered perfectly reasonable by them. This is no more than they claim for themselves. Members of the old ritualistic churches should not ridicule us for professing this experience; for they themselves profess to have received it in baptism or in confirmation. Christians who believe that we are sanctified only at death should find no fault with those who claim to have received that experience earlier in life.

RESULTS OF THE REMOVAL OF INBRED SIN

Harm has been done by leading young converts to expect emotional and ecstatic experiences which may not be realized. In estimating the meaning of deliverance from inbred sin it is important to remember that this does not mean a deliverance from human nature itself as God first gave it to man. A study of biology reveals the fact that the very existence of man's life is dependent upon a few very positive urges. We might liken these to the cylinders in an automobile engine. The most important of these urges are (1) hunger for food, (2) a desire for human fellowship, (3) the sex urge, (4) escape from pain, (5) the urge to self-fulfillment—achievement, (6) self-preservation. If you have seen a different way of arranging or naming these urges it is immaterial; for uniformity is not essential here.

These are the general principles and, for the most part, all sin in a person's life takes place through the abuse and misuse of these urges. This fact is so certain that it has led many Christians to identify these urges with the nature of sin itself. Consequently, they suppose that deliverance from the nature of sin means deliverance from these urges. Now it is obvious that deliverances from these urges would end any person's life unless he were confined in an institution under expert, professional care. Therefore it is important to remember that deliverance from inbred sin cannot possibly mean destruction of these instincts by which human life is maintained and made vigorous. A destruction of carnality can be nothing other than the cleansing of these urges from the fever of sin, so that they will be more amenable to the control of the Christian conscience and will.

It is well also to remember that even the experience of entire sanctification is the endowment of a vast spiritual potentiality which will be realized in each given individual only in part, and quite largely in proportion to his light and his spiritual sensitivity. This is a fact of the Christian life which multitudes of Christians ought to know. It is natural for us to judge the size of a man's gift by the use to which he has put it, but that is not a reasonable conclusion to make. Two young men each inherit a million dollars. One manages to preserve his fortune intact and live upon the income thereof without ever making any impression of any kind on the world. Another seems to thrill every dollar with the vitality of his own vigorous personality so much that he multiplies his fortune manyfold and becomes known to the world far and wide. Obviously, we cannot judge the size of the gift they received by the use which they made of it.

Two boys are born with great natural ability—practically equal, yet one turns his attention to the humble work of his own community and the other develops his ability in such a way as to achieve world fame. So it is with Christians who receive the priceless gifts of God. It is unreasonable to demand the same astonishing world-shaking fame of all sanctified believers. The majority of even that famous company of the twelve apostles lived obscure and hidden lives and died unknown to men, except that their names alone appeared in that immortal company. Yet we have scriptural evidence that these were men of pure heart, soundest consecration, perfect in love, wholly acceptable in the kindly eyes of the Son of Man. In heaven their crown will not be dimmed in anywise by the humility and obscurity of their gentle and self-effacing lives.

Perhaps our Christianity needs more of a consecration to anonymity, more of willingness to be the least in the kingdom of heaven. Purity and humility are the passions of the saints.

VII.
THE BAPTISM OF THE HOLY SPIRIT

In the ancient church believers were baptized, and after baptism hands were laid upon them for the reception of the Holy Ghost. In New Testament times, they were taught that the sinner was regenerated, justified, converted, or saved before his baptism, and his baptism was a symbol of that conversion. Later, hands were laid upon him, in order that he might experience the second crisis. Then laid they their hands on them, and they received the Holy Ghost" (Acts 8:17).

At Ephesus, "when Paul had laid his hands upon them, the Holy Ghost came on them" (Acts 19:6). At Damascus, "Ananias went his way, and entered into the house; and putting his hands on him said, Brother Saul, the Lord, even Jesus, that appeared unto thee in the way as thou earnest, hath sent me, that thou mightest receive thy sight, and be filled with the Holy Ghost" (Acts 9:17).

Sometimes the Holy Ghost fell without the laying on of hands, but subsequent to conversion: "And there appeared unto them cloven tongues like as of fire, and it sat upon each of them. And they were all filled with the Holy Ghost" (Acts 2:3-4). The household of Cornelius received the same blessing in the same way: "While Peter yet spake these words, the Holy Ghost fell on all them which heard the word. And they of the circumcision which believed were astonished, as many as came with Peter, because that on the Gentiles also was poured out the gift of the Holy Ghost" (Acts 10:44).

In every one of these instances there is reasonable evidence that the persons thus baptized with the Holy Ghost were previously converted—were truly regenerated believers. The evidence of this is tedious to gather and present, but is obvious to any candid reader. Concerning the disciples before the day of Pentecost, no man would need fear to go to judgment with even less assurance of justification than they enjoyed. They were sons of God. "And he lifted up his eyes on his disciples, and said, Blessed be ye poor: for yours is the kingdom of God" (Luke 6:20). One of these disciples, the Apostle John, said: "He came unto his own, and his own received him not. But as many as received him, to them gave he power to become the sons of God, even to them that believe on his name: which were born, not of blood, nor of the will of the flesh, nor of the will of man, but of God" (John 1:11-13). "For it is not ye that speak, but the Spirit of your Father which speaketh in you" (Matt. 10:20).

Even at that time, Christ had power to forgive sin: "And behold, they brought to him a man sick of the palsy, lying on a bed: and Jesus seeing their faith said unto the sick of the palsy: Son, be of good cheer; thy sins be forgiven thee" (Matt. 9:2). Of the woman who washed his feet, Christ said: "Wherefore I say unto thee, Her sins, which are many, are forgiven; for she loved much....And He said unto her, Thy sins are forgiven. And they that sat at meat with him began to say within themselves, Who is this that forgiveth sins also?" (Luke 7:47-49). "Notwithstanding in this rejoice not, that the spirits are subject unto you; but rather rejoice, because your names are written in heaven" (Luke 10:20).

The disciples were acknowledged as saved by Christ: "Now ye are clean through the word which I have spoken unto you. I am the vine, ye are the branches: He that abideth in me, and I in him, the same bringeth forth much fruit: for without me ye can do nothing" (John 15:3, 5).

If they were in Christ they had no condemnation: "There is therefore now no condemnation to them which are in Christ Jesus" (Rom. 8:1); "Therefore if any man be in Christ, he is a new creature: old things are passed away; behold, all things are become new" (II Cor. 5:17); "Whosoever abideth in him sinneth not" (I John 3:6).

Christ had called the apostles to preach before they were baptized by the Holy Spirit on the Day of Pentecost. "And Jesus, walking by the Sea of Galilee, saw two brethren, Simon called Peter, and Andrew his brother...and he said unto them, Follow me, and I will make you fishers of men" (Matt. 4:18-19). "Ye have not chosen me, but I have chosen you, and ordained you, that ye should go and bring forth fruit" (John 15:16). "These twelve Jesus sent forth, and commanded them....And as ye go, preach, saying, The kingdom of heaven is at hand. Heal the sick, cleanse the lepers, raise the dead, cast out devils" (Matt. 10:5, 7-8).

It is certainly straining a point to say that men called and sent by Christ to preach and cast out devils were not even converted themselves. These God-called men "went out, and preached that men should repent. And they cast out many devils, and anointed with oil many that were sick, and healed them" (Mark 6:12-13).

To these converted men Christ said, "I will pray the Father, and he shall give you another Comforter, that he may abide with you forever, even the Spirit of truth WHOM THE WORLD CANNOT RECEIVE" (John 14:16-17). Notice this is an experience that sinners cannot obtain. The world cannot receive the Spirit, although the world can receive salvation, or justification, by faith. "But the Comforter, which is the Holy Ghost, whom the Father will send in my name, he shall teach you all things" (14:26). "For if I go not away, the Comforter will not come unto you; but if I depart, I will send him unto you" (16:7).

Long before these men received the baptism of the Holy Ghost Jesus said of them: "If ye were of the world, the world would love his own: but because ye are not of the world, but I have chosen you out of the world, therefore the world hateth you" (John 15:19); "They are not of the world, even as I am not of the world" (17:14).

Although the disciples were regenerated men before Pentecost, they were not yet perfected in love. They had tormenting fear. "Why are ye fearful, O ye of little faith?" (Matt. 8:26). In the hour of Christ's passion "they all forsook him, and fled" (Mark 14:50). They were afraid when they saw Christ walking on the sea (John 6:19). Frivolous people will regard these references as trivial, but it must be remembered that the New Testament is a very brief book and every one of these historical notes was put in for a special purpose. In this case they seem to connect with the words of the Apostle John after he had received the baptism of the Holy Ghost and spent a long life in the serenity of that "perfect love," when he wrote: "There is no fear in love; but perfect love casteth out fear: because fear hath torment. He that feareth is not made perfect in love" (I John 4:18).

These regenerated men personally called by Christ to preach the gospel were not yet wholly sanctified, and for these Christ prayed: "I pray for them: I pray not for the world, but for them which thou hast given me; for they are thine. Sanctify them through thy truth: thy word is truth" (John 17:9, 17). The Apostle John often uses the word truth as a synonym for reality. The meaning of the passage is: Make them holy in reality, as they are already holy in name, or ceremonially.

Some people have stumbled over the fact that some of the modern versions read "consecrate" instead of "sanctify." This, however, is due to a common misunderstanding of the word *consecrate*. Here it is synonymous with the word *sanctify*. The first definition which Webster gives of consecrate is: "To make, or declare, sacred or holy." Notice that in the modern texts it is not said that the apostles should consecrate themselves, an expression conformable to the popular meaning of consecrate. On the contrary, the modern versions generally read "consecrate them" (imperative mood). That is, God is asked to consecrate them, and that is exactly the same meaning as that of the versions which say "sanctify them."

However, some of the most scholarly of the modern versions read: "Make them holy," e. g., Weymouth, and Ferrar Fenton. Use of the term consecrate here would not disturb a scholar in the least, for he would understand clearly that when God consecrates a man that means he sanctifies him. It is a great pity, however, that the scholarly translators have caused so many readers to stumble by using a common religious word in a way unfamiliar to laymen.

When Christ says that he consecrates himself, it means that he devotes himself to die on the cross and to suffer for the sanctification of believers, as well as the salvation of sinners. These prayers of Christ for his disciples and his accompanying promises to them received their fulfillment on the Day of Pentecost, when they were all filled with the Holy Ghost (Acts 2:4). This Holy Spirit is the sanctifier: "Being sanctified by the Holy Ghost" (Rom. 15:16).

Regarding Cornelius, we have no doubt that he was like all others on the record—a saved man before he was baptized with the Holy Spirit. The evidence would completely convince any believer not prejudiced by a dogmatic bias. Briefly we note a few facts about him. He was God-fearing and godly (devout—*eusebes)*, praying "to God alway" (Acts 10:2). If one should hear a minister speak thus of a dead man at his funeral would not he assume that the minister thought the man to have been saved? Cornelius saw a vision (Acts 10:3, 30-31) just as did Paul at his conversion (9:3-6). In this vision he asked for guidance, as did Paul. The heavenly visitant assured Cornelius that his prayers had been heard—he obtained a definite and an unquestioned answer to prayer. How could he still be a sinner? All the evidence indicates that Cornelius was a convert of Hellenic Judaism, and like multitudes of others, had not become an orthodox Pharisaic Jew.

Why all this repetitious insistence in Luke's narrative emphasizing the godliness of Cornelius? Is it necessary for a man to be godly in order to repent and become converted? Far from it. Jesus called publicans and sinners. He came not to call the righteous, but sinners to repentance. Cornelius did not repent at this time; he was a devout man. A man does not need to be devout in order to become converted. But it is necessary for a man to be saved in order to be worthy of receiving the baptism of the Holy Ghost. And Luke is doing his utmost to prove that Cornelius and his friends were already saved, and thus prepared and worthy to receive the Holy Spirit, "whom the world cannot receive" (John 14:17).

All other examples noted in the Scriptures, except Paul (Acts 9:17-18), were baptized before they received the Holy Spirit. In the case of Cornelius, the baptism of the Spirit came first to convince Jewish Christians that these Gentiles were previously accepted of God, as Peter had expressly stated (10:35). In the case of the others whose experience is recorded, while the total number is few, the fact that in every case they were already Christian believers, as attested by their baptism, is overwhelming evidence that the baptism of the Holy Spirit is an experience reserved for Christians only and is not bestowed upon the world.

The people of Samaria believed in Christ (Acts 8:12), experienced a perfectly amazing revival (vss. 6-8), and were baptized in water (vs. 12). Then in order to emphasize the distinction between the two crises, (vs. 26) two other men came to lead the people into this second crisis of Spirit baptism (vss. 14-17) subsequent to their conversion and water baptism.

The disciples at Ephesus were old believers, who had not—like many today—understood their privilege of receiving Spirit baptism. Even here Paul insisted on water baptism first.

These numerous cases where people were first baptized with water present an unbreakable argument for the second crisis of salvation. First, nearly all evangelical Christians, in America at least, believe that water baptism is a symbol of spiritual regeneration and that baptism follows regeneration. Now, if water baptism follows regeneration it stands to reason that people baptized with the Holy Spirit subsequent to their water baptism were necessarily baptized with the Spirit after their conversion. Such were most of the cases in the New Testament (for example, Acts 2:4; 8:16-17; 19:5-6).

However, the argument is fully as strong in the case of Sacramentarian Christians who believe that penitents are regenerated in the very act of baptism and by means of baptism as a sacrament. For if this is true, then the baptism of the Spirit occurs after a lapse of time subsequent to the regeneration in water baptism. And this lapse of time might as well be several years as several minutes. This is exactly what the Catholic church holds; for confirmation is a continuation of the form of laying on hands for the baptism of the Holy Spirit as recorded in Acts. (See references in *Deeper Experiences of Famous Christians*, by J. G. Lawson, pp. 46, 50 ff.)

That the interval of time between the water baptism and the baptism of the Holy Spirit may be stretched out for years is the teaching and practice of the Catholic church. In ancient times, when the church baptized adults they proceeded at once to lay hands upon them and to pray for the baptism of the Holy Spirit, in obedience to the example of the apostles given in the Book of Acts. Later on, when the baptism of infants was introduced, it was thought inappropriate to expect an infant to receive the baptism of the Holy Spirit, with all that vast blessing implies of purity and perfection. Consequently, the Catholic church, judging the interval of time between the baptizing with water and the baptism of the Spirit to be unimportant, postpones the spiritual baptism until the child comes to the age of accountability, sometime between its twelfth and fourteenth years.

This ceremony of the reception of the Holy Spirit in the Catholic church is called confirmation, following the statement of Paul in II Corinthians: "Now he which stablisheth us with you in Christ, and hath anointed us, is God; who hath also sealed us, and given the earnest of the Spirit in our hearts" (1:21-22). The Latin version reads *confirmat* (or stablisheth) us.

In this way it can be demonstrated that the doctrine of two definite crises in the work of salvation has been exactly the same in form in the teaching of the historic Christian church for nineteen hundred years. We believe completely in the doctrine of the Catholic church that salvation consists of two crises; first, regeneration; and, second, an anointing of the Spirit. The only difference is that we believe that these experiences must be more than formal ceremonies and must be guaranteed by something more definite than the ritual of the church, namely, by the witness of the Holy Spirit in the heart of the seeker. But we insist that this doctrine of the second crisis has been taught *in form* throughout the whole history of the church. What we now urge is a recovery of the meaning and spirit of that teaching in living Christian experience.

The accounts given in the Book of Acts concerning the baptism of the Holy Spirit have been a source of confusion and bewilderment to the technical theologians from time out of mind. They described a condition of affairs which had not only gone out of existence but had actually been forgotten. They were like the bones of some ancient dinosaur found by an ignorant man in thick layers of heavy rock. How they ever got there would be a source of puzzlement to him as long as he lived. The old-time orthodox theologians invented a clever little theory which relieved them of the necessity of any realistic interpretation of these records. They said that the apostolic age was an age of miracles, when anything might happen; but no one is under an obligation to explain a miracle. "Besides," they said, "it never can happen again." Therefore all these strange fossils in the solid rock of Holy Scripture really required no explanation and admitted no application to our own time.

No one could be more hostile to modern religious liberalism than I am. Nevertheless, common honesty demands that we conservatives concede to the liberal critics an honest willingness to construe the stories in the apostolic records in a completely realistic manner. Anything that could happen then could happen today under similar conditions, so they admit. The tragedy of such liberal interpretation, however, is that they do not believe that the baptism of the Spirit recorded in Acts represents anything more than the hysterical excitement of ignorant men in a superstitious age. Insofar as the liberal critics allow any real operation of the Spirit in the event, they tend to follow the orthodox theory that there was something special about it not applicable to our times.

We refuse to accept either of these interpretations. We cannot believe that these numerous baptisms of the Spirit recorded in the Book of Acts are without meaning. These stories are there for our inspiration and example. Even the early Wesleyan theologians were so far misled by the technical theologians that they failed to put proper emphasis on the baptism of the Holy Spirit. They tended to interpret sanctification as a crisis experience, it is true, but found most of their proof texts in other parts of the New Testament. The technical theologians have been inclined to minify the spiritual application of these stories to our own time by pressing the idea that this baptism of the Spirit was something special for that age, in which the people received something unique—special gifts such as tongues and the like. This argument is largely canceled out by the fact that the scriptural description of that baptism of the Holy Spirit specifically describes it as a purification of the heart. Peter was a better theologian than any modern critic, and that is the way he described the baptism of the Holy Ghost—as "purifying their hearts by faith" (Acts 15:9). This expression—"purifying the heart"—proves beyond cavil that the baptism of the Holy Spirit is indeed a redemptive work of grace intimately linked with the atonement of Christ. There is a second crisis of salvation.

VIII.
THE WORK OF THE HOLY SPIRIT

Careless readers of the Bible have attributed to the plan of salvation a simplicity which it does not have. Just as we find depth and complexity when we attempt a close study of nature, so we likewise find many deep truths when we seek to study the Bible and the plan of salvation. One of these truths is that the Holy Spirit has more than one "office work."

This is illustrated by the case of a man who is a judge and a physician. As a physician he would seek to save a criminal's life and as a judge he might sentence him to death. There is nothing contradictory in the two offices or professions combined in one man. That is the explanation of the problem concerning Christ's promising to send his Holy Spirit when throughout the Old Testament there are numerous references to prove that he has always been in the world. Christ sent him in the special office work of the sanctifier to perfect the church on the Day of Pentecost and to dwell in it in sanctifying power forever. The multiple work of the Holy Spirit in human life is set forth in scriptural symbols and there is value in them.

AIR AS AN EMBLEM OF THE SPIRIT

When men began to talk about spiritual things they had to use physical things to illustrate their meaning. We say we grasp a subject when we mean, not that we take hold of it with the hand, but with the mind. In this way, the word air came to be used for spirit from the most ancient time. In Genesis 1:2 the Hebrew says the *"ruach* of God brooding on the waters." Here *ruach* is literally the "breath of God," and the text means that the Spirit of God brooded over the chaos of the ancient world like a bird brooding over her eggs. And this is the way that God's Spirit has brooded over the souls of all men throughout all times, from the dawn of their existence until their death, or until they had grieved him away forever, if possible. It was this Spirit of God that breathed life into the first man (Gen. 2:7). The Hebrew here says *chayyim*—lives—not one life, but many, all merging into one personality like many little flames merging into one bonfire.

"The breath of the Almighty hath given me life" (Job 33:4). Prophesy unto the wind, prophesy, son of man, and say to the wind, Thus saith the Lord God; Come from the four winds, O breath, and breathe upon these slain, that they may live" (Ezek. 37:9). These texts indicate how the Holy Spirit works to create life, and this truth is climaxed by the teaching of Jesus concerning the work of the Spirit in producing the new birth. "Except a man be born of water and of the Spirit, he cannot enter into the kingdom of God....The wind bloweth where it listeth, and thou hearest the sound thereof, but canst not tell whence it cometh, and whither it goeth: so is every one that is born of the Spirit" (John 3:5, 8).

And so we see that the work of the Spirit is not confined to the experience of entire sanctification. In fact, the Holy Spirit begins to work with men long before they are ever converted. It is he who convicts men of sin and makes them have a desire to find God. "When he is come, he will reprove the world of sin" (John 16:8). That reproof produces what we call "conviction of sin," whenever it is heeded by the soul.

Some holiness teachers hold that the office work of the Spirit as breather of life is confined to a preparation for, and experience of, regeneration, having no place in the work of entire sanctification. But I think differently: I believe that the idea of a creative force of spiritual power is conveyed in the first record of Spirit baptism given in the second chapter of Acts. At that time, "suddenly there came a sound from heaven as of a rushing mighty wind, and it filled all the house where they were sitting" (Acts 2:2). Some say this was merely the sound. I believe that sound was not a false appearance, but denoted the presence of the creative breath of God as it was felt on the dry bones of Ezekiel's army and upon the lifeless body of the first man. This must needs be so if our doctrine of the restoration of the divine image is correct; for it is this creative breath of the Spirit which creates anew the perfect image of God in the heart of a redeemed man, just as it created the image of God in Adam at the dawn of his existence. This is what Christ meant when he said, "I am come that they might have life, and that they might have it more abundantly" (John 10:10). This is the abundant life, imparted by the breath of God in the experience of entire sanctification.

THE HOLY SPIRIT AS FIRE

From immemorial ages the wondering eyes of simpleminded men have gazed at the mysterious movement of a flame of fire in a vain effort to explore its hidden secret. And even in this scientific age, when men know the name and meaning of the chemical change involved, they still must feel baffled by the fact that they have only given a technical description of their ignorance. Fire has seemed to all men as a fit emblem of the nature of God. Man's best friend, heating his building, cooking his food, making life possible in cold climates—no wonder St. Francis called it Brother Fire. Fire has, nevertheless, demanded of man certain cautions and respect; for it has always been capable of striking back at him with withering power whenever he treats it lightly.

And it so happens that nearly all men who have ever believed in God have been led to think of him somewhat in the same paradoxical vein. They love him, they recognize his friendship and the benefits of his aid, and they fear him in recognition of the fact that he always holds the power to visit with stern rebuke every lack of respect that might be shown him. So it happens that throughout the Bible fire appears repeatedly as an emblem of the presence of God. The Old

Testament prophets saw God in visions as "a great cloud, and a fire enfolding itself" (Ezek. 1:4). Moses saw God in a burning bush of flame (Exod. 3:2-4).

This fire teaches many truths; perhaps the most important is that of cleansing. The baptism of the Holy Spirit fell upon the disciples on the day of Pentecost as "cloven tongues like as of fire" (Acts 2:3). And the cleansing nature of this fire is set forth by Malachi: "He is like a refiner's fire, and like fullers' soap: and he shall sit as a refiner and purifier of silver: and he shall purify the sons of Levi, and purge them as gold and silver, that they may offer unto the Lord an offering in righteousness" (Mal. 3:2-3).

Nowadays gold is purified by chemical processes, but in Bible times it was purified by fire, which melted the ore together so that the dross came to the top. The dross was then skimmed off and cast aside, leaving only the pure gold, in which the workman could see his face reflected. Such is the work of Christ when he purifies hearts in the baptism of the Holy Ghost and fire. This is the fire promised in the preaching of John: "He that cometh after me...shall baptize you with the Holy Ghost, and with fire: whose fan is in his hand, and he will thoroughly purge his floor, and gather his wheat into the garner; but he will burn up the chaff with unquenchable fire" (Matt. 3:11-12). This was the fire Isaiah experienced when, bewildered and humbled by the stupendous vision of God, he confessed the uncleanness of a religious man and immediately experienced purification by fire: "Then flew one of the seraphims unto me, having a live coal in his hand, which he had taken with the tongs from off the altar: and he laid it upon my mouth, and said, Lo, this hath touched thy lips; and thine iniquity is taken away, and thy sin purged" (Isa. 6:6-7).

Fire not only symbolizes cleansing and purity but it is also an emblem of energy and power: "Ye shall receive power, after that the Holy Ghost is come upon you: and ye shall be witnesses unto me...unto the uttermost part of the earth" (Acts 1:8). A good concordance will reveal to the student very many references concerning the power of the Holy Spirit in the heart.

Many people misunderstand this power, thinking it ought to be a destructive force that shatters body and mind in some kind of hysterical shaking and insane behavior. The text just quoted will dissipate these misconceptions by showing that the principal function of the power of the Spirit is to enable one to witness for Christ; that is, witness by holy life and by faithful and persuasive words as one whose speech is "alway with grace, seasoned with salt, that ye may know how ye ought to answer every man" (Col. 4:6). "For God hath not given us the spirit of fear; but of power, and of love, and of a sound mind" (II Tim. 1:7). Some sixteen hundred years ago, the great scholars of the church began to lay down the principle that the work of the Holy Spirit, purely and of itself, would be to strengthen and tranquilize the mind and reason. It may be that some great saint has on occasion given away to hysterical frenzy; but if so, it was a weakness of human flesh similar to that weakness to which the saints are always exposed. But the highest manifestation of the Spirit's power is in love and a sound mind. Moses talked to God face to face, but he never went into a trance. Jesus was the supreme prophet of all times, yet he did not "cry, nor lift up, nor cause his voice to be heard in the streets." He was never in a trance and never for any moment did he become hysterical and display signs of insanity. He is our supreme example.

THE HOLY SPIRIT AS WATER

Many passages of the Bible set forth water as an emblem of the Holy Spirit. "I will pour water upon him that is thirsty, and floods upon the dry ground: I will pour my spirit upon thy seed, and my blessing upon thine offspring: and they shall spring up as among the grass, as willows by the watercourses" (Isa. 44:3-4). Here water represents the refreshing and stimulating power of the Spirit. "Christ also loved the church, and gave himself for it; that he might sanctify and cleanse it with the washing of water by the word, that he might present it to himself a glorious church, not having spot, or wrinkle, or any such thing; but that it should be holy and without blemish" (Eph. 5:25-26). Here water represents the cleansing work of the Spirit in washing away all the remains of inbred sin.

> The negative side of sanctification is that of emptying, removing, destroying the carnal mind. The positive side of sanctification involves filling the purified heart with light and love and multiplying within it the graces of the Spirit and enjoying those graces. Now so far as I can discover, this is just the significance of the two sanctifying emblems of fire and water. The fire represents purity with the idea of destruction, of consuming;

water represents the idea of purity with the positive upbuilding of the soul in truth and strength and love.[1]

THE HOLY SPIRIT AS OIL

"But the anointing which ye have received of him abideth in you, and ye need not that any man teach you: but as the same anointing teacheth you of all things, and is truth, and is no lie, and even as it hath taught you, ye shall abide in him" (I John 2:27). Oil had a value to the ancients of Palestine beyond our conception in this modern day. In that age men had not learned how to preserve food for livestock so as to keep them throughout the winter. Consequently, fat meat food was considered a great luxury. Because the olive tree took many years to grow it was considered an emblem of peace. Such factors as these contributed to make any kind of oil seem much more important then than now. Perfumed oil was also esteemed a great luxury. For such reasons as these, priests and kings were anointed with oil in elaborate ceremony to signify the enduement of power and privilege which were granted by their office. Prophets, too, were anointed for the prophetic office. A book could be written upon the meaning of anointing in the Scripture. "Oil in the Old Testament appears as the symbol of the communication of the Spirit."[2]

Even the word "Christ" simply means "anointed," as the Scriptures have said: "The Spirit of the Lord God is upon me; because the Lord hath anointed me to preach good tidings

1. E. D. Watson, *Coals of Fire,* p. 102.
2. Gustav Friedrich Oehler, *Theology of the Old Testament,* p. 273.

unto the meek; he hath sent me to bind up the brokenhearted, to proclaim liberty to the captives, and the opening of the prison to them that are bound" (Isa. 61:1). "God anointed Jesus of Nazareth with the Holy Ghost and with power" (Acts 10:38). The anointing of the Old Testament, therefore seems to signify the enduement of authority to rule (the king), to minister (the priest), and to teach (the prophet). Translated into the framework of New Testament ideals, this would signify the noble character of divine self-control, the capacity to lead men to God, and joyous insight into the truth; for the New Testament saints are kings and priests unto God (Rev. 1:6), and they have an anointing that teaches them.

IX.
ENTIRE SANCTIFICATION AS A BUNDLE OF POSSIBILITIES

The doctrine of entire sanctification has been preached on the American continent in the Wesleyan tradition as the second work of grace, or as a second crisis in Christian experience, for about two hundred years; and while doubtless its opponents would admit that it has on occasion produced astonishing results, an unbiased and fair-minded critic must admit that many of its most sincere teachers and professors have felt deep and widespread disappointment with the results in their own individual experience and observation. In many instances there has been a gap in practice between what the best teachers promised and the actual results obtained by the average Christian who claimed the experience.

How shall we explain this simple, but undeniable, fact? First of all, it might be said that even if it were a matter of secular discipline of the mind, results would naturally be widely different. One man studies art intently and gets very little out of it. Some students will tell you that they got nothing from their mathematics teacher. Others found their history course nearly worthless. Men who have taken courses in memory training have forgotten to put on their overcoats when they left the class the last time. And no doubt even a few students of courses in winning friends and influencing people have finished quite as tactless and as provocative in manner as any rugged individualist could wish. It is just not in the nature of things for the minds of all men to respond to mental or spiritual stimuli and experiences in the same manner.

Therefore we make bold to say that even on the lower level of secular psychology we are not justified in condemning a doctrine or mental discipline because it does not produce uniform results in the various types of mind which are subjected to it. But entire sanctification is not a secular doctrine; it is by definition an experience of the introduction of new power and grace into human life. If it be true that many who have sought this experience have failed to realize their expectations, we have a puzzling problem. What is the use of preaching about mountaintop experiences and fullness of joy, when multitudes of those who profess entire sanctification seem to suffer even more than their neighbors? Why preach about inrushing oceans of crystal power and victory when we know so many sanctified people who are struggling, perplexed, confused, and anxious, apparently just like other men?

Among orthodox teachers the stock answer to this question has been that these suffering people were not really wholly sanctified. Then we have added to the perplexity and sorrow of these earnest people by accusing them of hypocrisy, thus placing them under a strain of prayer and ascetic effort to lift themselves to some imaginary type of blessedness.

To me there seems to be a better way, in which we shall be realistically honest with ourselves and perfectly candid in our report to the outside world.

Many seekers for the experience have misunderstood the meaning of the cleansing of our nature and the destruction of carnality. They have taken this experience to signify that the natural appetites, by which physical life is preserved and continued, will be eradicated and destroyed by entire sanctification. A little thought would convince anyone of the impossibility of the realization of such an experience. Without hunger the body would waste away and die. Without sex appetite the race would cease from the earth. Without fear men would utterly destroy the life of mankind from the earth. It is the exaggeration and feverish poisoning of these impulses which is cured by the baptism of the Holy Ghost.

While it is correct that the instinctive pattern of holy living is restored to the heart by the restoration of the image of God in sanctification, it is important to remember that the possession of human intelligence modifies the deterministic control of instinct in the case of a human being. Here is an illustration. A hungry bird will carry a luscious morsel of food to deposit in the mouth of its nestling. Now it is easy for the bird to do this, because it has an instinctive pattern of behavior wrought in its very nature and it has no intelligence sufficient to balance its own impulse of hunger against the instinctive urge to feed its young. But if that bird were suddenly gifted with human intelligence, naturally it would begin to think about the comparative advantages of feeding its young or of satisfying its own hunger. And we may be sure that to go hungry to feed its young would be a harder thing for the bird to do if it were possessed of human intelligence. And we may also be sure that many birds would obey the impulse to satisfy their individual hunger rather than the instinctive urge to feed their young.

I emphasize this point, for so far as I know, it has never before been introduced into the literature of the doctrine of entire sanctification. Yet a little consideration will prove that it is true. Further thought will make it very apparent why even a sanctified man, who has the instinctive pattern of holiness restored to his heart, will often, if not always, find a tension between his simple physical impulses and the organized pattern of religious instinct implanted into his nature by the grace of God. We hope that earnest Christians will ponder this explanation well as a solution of one of the most troublesome problems of the sanctified life and of the origin of sin in a holy being.

Too many people have neglected the *continuous response* which a sanctified man must make to the indwelling grace of God. Jesus explained it all in the Parable of the Sower. The seed sown represents the whole work of grace in the heart, and thus could be applied to the baptism of the Holy Ghost, the enduement of spiritual power; although the seed is all very much alike, it does not produce anything like uniform results. Jesus explains carefully that its historical outcome shows returns of thirty, sixty, and a hundredfold. (See Matt. 13:8.) Here Jesus inferentially rebukes all this expectation that the baptism of the Holy Spirit would produce uniform results in all who experience it. And it is important to remember that the field which produced only a thirtyfold increase was not condemned as an apostate and useless piece of ground. It was in its way an example, if not of the best, at least of the satisfactory Christian experience. Notice that Christ teaches with crystal clearness here that the returns are not in anywise limited by the goodness of the seed or the generosity with which it is sown; they are limited by the nature of the soil itself. It is a great mistake for teachers of the doctrine of entire sanctification to infer that all its possessors will realize its possibilities a hundredfold. Doubtless that is a goal to be sought, but failure to realize it should not be condemned as apostasy.

One could extend this discussion by many similar analogies. Back in the 1890s, a young man in Detroit saved and borrowed $20,000. This money he invested in the Ford Motor Company, and while he was still a comparatively young man he sold out his stock in that company for $33,000,000. At the very time that James Couzens invested $20,000 in the automobile business, other young men in Detroit were in possession of similar amounts of money. Their money was just as good. It was issued by Uncle Sam. It was in no way different from the money held by Mr. Couzens. But Mr. Couzens realized, perhaps, just about all the financial possibilities of his money, and most of the others failed to do so. Some made only reasonable gains; others lost all that they had. And so it is with the baptism of the Holy Spirit. A great deal depends upon how the individual uses the gift of the Spirit so freely given. Undoubtedly the possibilities are great, but those who receive should bestow more thought and prayer upon the realization of the vast potentialities of the gift.

SEEK NOT THE GIFT BUT THE GIVER

No apologies need to be made for presenting the baptism of the Holy Spirit, the experience of entire sanctification, as a gift. This is scriptural language. Moreover, it is borne out by numerous spiritual analogies in the parables of our Lord. It is of great importance that all who are concerned with this great truth should understand clearly and emphasize fully the fact that this is a very peculiar and unique gift. The gift of the Holy Spirit is not the gift of a thing, such as a bushel of wheat or a ton of dynamite or a million dollars. Such figures are not entirely inaccurate, because they do represent the truth that the gift of the Holy Spirit is an enduement of power that puts the soul in possession of enormous potentialities.

But we have never realized the meaning of entire sanctification so long as we think of it merely as a thing which does certain things. Rather, it is a man's personal experience in which he receives the gift of a person, not given as an ancient slaveowner would give away one of his slaves, but given as today a lover gives himself to his bride, or as a great man gives himself in warm and confiding friendship to another man whom he regards as morally worthy of that friendship.

Throughout this whole discussion we have found that most of our difficulties are relieved by thinking of our relationship to God as a personal one. Here the parables, analogies, and figures of religion come nearest to the absolute truth and are freest from the possibility of misunderstanding. If we think of the baptism of the Holy Ghost as the special, kindly, loving presentation of the Third Person of the Godhead to its recipients in the wealth of a rich and enduring friendship, we have solved most of the problems raised regarding the lack of uniformity in the results of this experience.

Here is a helpful illustration. Take the great industrial leaders and men of vast fortune. Although they are compelled to guard themselves against infringement upon their time by thousands of idle hangers-on and beggars of every description, it will generally remain true that each of them has a considerable number of friends to whom he continues to give himself throughout life. Let us study these friends as illustrations of the lack of uniformity in the sanctified experience. Among them, here and there, will be men who through this friendship have risen to places of enormous power and prestige in the American industrial world. The head of the great corporation has smiled upon them and they have become powerful executives and multimillionaires in their turn, and yet this head of the corporation has humble friends, some of whom perhaps are shabby men who have never known much success in life and whose only boast is that they are personal friends of the head of the corporation. They have the gift of the captain's friendship, but they have never been able to utilize the possibilities of that friendship to anything like the extent which other men have. Doubtless, like all other parables, this parable can be misconstrued. We can say that the captain of industry was unfair to his humble friends. Ruling out that possibility, is it not reasonable to believe that many of his humble friends were well known by him to be incapable of the heavy burdens of responsibility which his power made it possible for him to bestow, but which his wisdom and friendship would not allow him to impose upon a weak friend? If the possibilities of friendship with a captain of industry are so vast and yet so variously realized in practice, is it any wonder that the baptism of the Holy Ghost, the gift of the Comforter, also presents a bundle of possibilities which few men have ever realized in anything but the smallest way? Lack of this complete realization should not be construed as apostasy from the faith, or hypocrisy in the life. As a sanctified man surveys the possibilities of a life in holiness, it should be an encouragement to possess the land.

FEATURES OF THE VICTORIOUS LIFE

Having shown clearly that not all sanctified people realize the possibilities which the experience holds, and guarding against fanaticism and pharisaism on the one hand, and doubt, anxiety, and self-condemnation on the other, it is well to make an optimistic view of the glorious possibilities of faith in the life of holiness opened up to the believer in the experience of entire sanctification. Remember, these are possibilities whose lack of realization should inspire one to more ardent zeal, rather than create a sense of failure and guilt. As we unfold a map of the mountains of Canaan, it is not for anyone to ask who lives on such a high plane as that, but rather to say, "By the grace of God that is my inheritance, and I will realize it more and more as long as I live."

THE BAPTISM OF THE HOLY GHOST GIVES POWER

Many years ago I read in a religious periodical an article that emphasized the fact that Christians should not pray for power, but pray first of all for purity; for when purity of heart is realized then power will naturally come and that power will be useful and a blessing. Though this is a good truth to remember, we must not forget that one of the most outstanding features of the promised baptism of the Holy Spirit was an enduement of power: "Tarry ye in the city of Jerusalem, until ye be endued with power from on high" (Luke 24:49). "Ye shall receive power after that the Holy Ghost is come upon you" (Acts 1:8).

Perhaps this "power" has created more confusion of thought than any other word in the teaching of this doctrine. First of all, we should remember that it is certainly not power to do just anything a man might wish to do. It is not power to make money; it is not power to avoid suffering; it is not power to bend others to our own will; it is not power to conquer our enemies nor to amass wealth. It is not intellectual power, which makes a man a scholar or a brilliant genius. It is not necessarily power to speak with eloquence and invincible persuasion. It is certainly not such power as Samson had, which made him able to carry the gates of Gath upon his back and to push the temple of Dagon over by physical force.

To define the power is by no means to deny it. A suggestion as to the kind of power it is may be seen in the text cited from Acts, which continues as follows: "And ye shall be witnesses unto me both in Jerusalem, and in all Judea, and in Samaria, and unto the uttermost part of the earth" (1:8). That seems to answer our question. The power received by the soul at Pentecost is the power to witness for Christ. Eventually this involves a good many things. It involves the power to live an upright, moral, and worthy life; for this is the first requisite to witnessing. The witness who appears in God's witness chair must be a man with clean hands and a pure heart and a reputation of honor and integrity before the world.

Furthermore, in such a life there must be power to overcome hatred, discouragement, bitterness, and the melancholy and gloom of life. "Great peace have they that love thy law: and nothing shall offend them." The exterior fabric of an honorable and noble life must constantly be rebuilt within by the beauty of a clean, courageous, and pure experience. This takes power.

This is a power which exalts a man above the baffling, frustrating circumstances of life. Undoubtedly this is a high claim, but nearly all of the great saints have testified to its reality. Madame Guyon, when in prison for Christ's sake, maintained a serene and cheerful heart and wrote a beautiful poem of herself as Christ's songbird shut up to sing for him. That takes power.

Incidental to this witnessing for Christ, there might be times when the Spirit's power would take the form of the prophetic gift of inspired preaching, in which the soul is caught up in rapture, filled with strange, lovely, bright and beautiful thoughts which are uttered with a passionate fervor that the oratory of trained speakers can never approach.

In all cases, this power is simply the manifestation of the Spirit's to aid us in witnessing for our beloved and exalted Lord. How foolish it is to think that this power should mean hysterical jumping and jerking and falling into trances. The Apostle Paul taught differently: "God has not given us the spirit of fear; but of power, and of love, and of a sound mind" (II Tim. 1:7). The power that accompanies Pentecost would rather strengthen the mind, quicken the intellect, warm the heart, elevate and intensify the intellectual capacity of its possessor. If in the Bible or in Christian history it could be shown that any spiritual person became hysterical and temporarily lost his reason, that would only prove how far that particular saint fell below the standard of spirituality lifted up by the Bible itself.

The greatest of all the Old Testament prophets, if we except John the Baptist, was Moses. He was the prophet whom the Messiah should most resemble (Deut. 18:15). Yet Moses never had one moment when his intellect was darkened by hysterical emotional excitement. He talked to God "face to face, as a man speaketh unto his friend" (Exod. 33:11), but always in the full blaze of a brilliant and clear-seeing intellect. Jesus is the supreme prophet of all time, both in ancient Israel and the Christian church, and he was the one of whom it was said, "He shall not strive, nor cry; neither shall any man hear his voice in the streets" (Matt. 12:19). Never once did he become hysterical, or unduly excited. Never once did he fall in unconsciousness. Always his mind was clear under the anointing of the Holy Ghost.

Perhaps we cannot too much exalt the blessed work of the Spirit, sending streams of healing, of peace, and of joy through what was once the wilderness of the human heart and making the desert blossom as the rose. Nevertheless, all Christians must be on guard against loving our Lord for his gift, rather than loving him as the giver. We love him for what he is, rather than for what he does for us. Remember, Judas was one disciple who prized Christ for what he thought he could get out of following him, rather than for what Christ was in himself. Thomas à Kempis, who died in 1471, wrote as follows:

> Many love Jesus so long as adversities happen not.
>
> Many praise and bless him, so long as they receive any consolations from him.
>
> But if Jesus hide himself, and leave them but a little while, they fall either into complaining, or into too much dejection of mind.
>
> But they who love Jesus for the sake of Jesus, and not for some special comfort of their own, bless him in all tribulation and anguish of heart, as well as in the state of highest comfort.
>
> And although he should never be willing to give them comfort, they notwithstanding would ever praise him, and wish to be always giving thanks.[1]

1. Thomas à Kempis, *The Imitation of Christ*, p. 104.

X.
THE MEANING OF HOLINESS

Sometimes it baffles the keenest intellect to formulate a clear-cut definition of many of the most common ideas in our minds. One reason why these ideas are so hard to define is because a few of them stand in a perfectly unique position, having no other thing like them to which they can be compared. Stop for a minute and try to define life. The attempt will baffle most people, and those who succeed in satisfying themselves will probably fail to satisfy many others.

Prof. Rudolph Otto has written a massive book on *The Idea of the Holy*, in which there is scarcely any mention of the kind of holiness with which we are concerned at this time. A brief reference to Dr. Otto's views will, however, contribute to a better understanding of the present discussion. Dr. Otto thinks that men first came to be aware of the presence of God as a tremendous mystery that aroused fear and trembling in all who gained any perception of its reality. In the thought of these ancient, savage men there was at first no distinction between God and devil; for they supposed that both good and injury might come from that brooding mystery of power which gave man his life without any choice or foreknowledge on man's part and suddenly withdrew that life like a man drawing his own breath back into his body.

Before we leave Dr. Otto we ought to be reminded that the historic development of religion always has been, and continues to be, along the lines he has indicated, and there is no other way to begin a genuinely religious experience but by evoking an awakening of the fear of God in a person's soul. "The fear of the Lord is the beginning of wisdom."

To understand the meaning of heart holiness, we must go back to this tremendous mystery of all ancient religions. In the Old Testament the holy thing is understood as the thing which belongs to God. Scan a good concordance and you note "holy ground," "holy gift," "holy garment," "holy thing," "holy crown," "a holy act," "holy anointing oil," and so we might go on at great length. Everything which belonged to the Tabernacle or the Temple belonged to God just as a man's house and furniture belong to that man. And everything which thus belonged to God was designated as holy.

HOLY AND MOST HOLY

At this point, there appears a paradoxical element in the idea of holiness which is likewise represented in the conception of personal property. That is, some things are more holy than others. From the standpoint of strict logic this is, of course, impossible. Since holy means the thing which belongs to God it is difficult to think of one thing as being more holy than another—that is, of God's owning one thing any more than he owns another. Nevertheless, this same idea occurs in our own ordinary conception of property. A multimillionaire owns a great factory and a vast estate. Literally, he owns everything in the factory and every blade of grass on the vast estate. But there are certain private belongings which seem to have a special reference to him. They are his clothing, his bed, or his spectacles. A guest in the mansion sits on chairs belonging to the master, uses furniture belonging to the master, reads books and papers belonging to the master, but he dare not intrude into the master's own bedroom where the master's own clothing is, carry the master's watch, and read the master's diary and personal account books. These are the master's peculiar, private, personal property. That is exactly the meaning of the text so often quoted: "Peculiar people, zealous of good works" (Tit. 2:14). That is also the meaning of the holy of holies in the ancient Temple. It was holier than the rest of the Temple because in a peculiar way it was the private, personal possession of God.

Meditation on this subject will help us to understand the meaning of entire sanctification. There is a sense in which every Christian is holy, as has been so urgently asserted against the holiness people. It might seem that if they are holy then there is no further holiness possible for them, but such people are exhorted to go on into the holy of holies. "Having therefore, brethren, boldness to enter into the holiest by the blood of Jesus, by a new and living way, which he hath consecrated for us through the veil, that is to say, his flesh; and having an high priest over the house of God; let us draw near with a true heart in full assurance of faith, having our hearts sprinkled from an evil conscience, and our bodies washed with pure water [our baptism]" (Heb. 10:19-22). Here the holy people are made holier; that is, they enter into the experience of entire sanctification. As regenerated Christians they belong to God in a general sense, but as those who have passed through the second crisis, they belong to God as a private, personal possession.

SANCTIFYING THE HOLY THINGS

There is a sense in which men sanctify a thing that is already holy by their deep, heartfelt acknowledgement of its holiness. This sense is common to Scripture, but it is seldom used in our ordinary religious language, as it is so liable to misunderstanding. Moses and Aaron were rebuked for not sanctifying God before Israel (Num. 20:12; 27:14). Israel was commanded to sanctify the Sabbath (Deut. 5:12). "The first-born…it is mine" (Exod. 13:2). The people were commanded to sanctify the house of the Lord God (II Chron. 29:5). And this idea of sanctifying God and his name is repeated elsewhere in the Old Testament. Even in the Lord's Prayer we pray "Hallowed be thy name," which means to sanctify the name of God. The only way in which the people can sanctify the Sabbath, the Temple, and the eternal God is by solemnly acknowledging the holiness in their own hearts. And it is by just such an act of consecration that the awakened believer consecrates himself to God in the second crisis of salvation.

TWO KINDS OF THINGS BELONG TO GOD

When the Israelites besieged the city of Jericho, Joshua devoted the entire place to God, declaring that not one person should escape, except the household of Rahab, and that not one article should be taken by the Israelites. "And the city shall be accursed, even it, and all that are therein, to the Lord: only Rahab the harlot shall live, she and all that are with her in the house, because she hid the messengers that we sent....Keep yourselves from the accursed thing, lest ye make yourselves accursed....But all the silver, and gold, and vessels of brass and iron, are consecrated unto the Lord: they shall come into the treasury of the Lord" (Josh. 6:17-19).

It is almost inevitable that we should think of the accursed thing as belonging to the devil, but if we study the Bible closely we begin to discern that the devil is a usurper in God's world and not much of anything belongs to him. However, the subject of the curse in the Old Testament is too extensive for full treatment here. There was a curse whose only meaning was harmful, but just now we are thinking of the devoted, *cherem,* that is illustrated by the passage before us. It is the thing which God owns but cannot use because it is unclean or otherwise objectionable to him. Everything in Jericho was devoted to God, but all was subject to destruction except the holy things—that is, the gold, silver, and such treasures as were not defiled by uncleanness, and therefore worthy of a place in the treasury of God. These were holy

(Josh. 6:19). The Hebrew word for consecrated is *qodesh*, which means holy.

It was the law in ancient Israel that "every firstling that cometh of a beast which thou hast; the males shall be the Lord's (Exod. 13:12). As a matter of course, therefore, the firstling of an ass would belong to the Lord according to the Law, but that animal was unfit for sacrifice. Therefore we read: "Every firstling of an ass thou shalt redeem with a lamb; and if thou wilt not redeem it, then thou shalt break his neck: and all the firstborn of man among thy children shalt thou redeem" (Exod. 13:13).

In other words, the ass belongs to God, but since he cannot use it, it must be destroyed unless it is redeemed. This same idea is repeated in Exodus 34:20. In Numbers we read: "The firstling of unclean beasts shalt thou redeem....But the firstling of a cow, or a firstling of a sheep, or the firstling of a goat, thou shalt not redeem; they are holy: thou shalt sprinkle their blood upon the altar, and shalt burn their fat for an offering made by fire, for a sweet savor unto the Lord" (Num. 18:15-17). In the Book of Leviticus we have the proposition laid down that "the firstling of the beasts, which should be the Lord's firstling, no man shall sanctify it" (Lev. 27:26). The reason no man could consecrate, or sanctify, a firstling was because it already belonged to God and could not, in the strictest sense of the word, be consecrated.

NO SINNER CAN CONSECRATE

This brings us up to the proposition that, strictly speaking, no sinner can ever consecrate himself to God. Following the scriptural line we have just studied, we see why this must be so—because every sinner already belongs to God, not as holy, but on the accursed side of the ledger: "Behold, all souls are mine; as the soul of the father, so also the soul of the son is mine: the soul that sinneth, it shall die" (Ezek. 18:4).

Every sinner in this world belongs to God, but, being unclean, he is on the accursed side and as such there is no hope for him except that he shall be redeemed like the unclean animals of the Mosaic dispensation. Of course, the unclean animals of the Old Testament could not be changed so as to become clean and fit for an offering but the sinner is changed—he is born again, made a new man in Christ Jesus, and as such he then comes to the place where he can consecrate himself and become a living sacrifice. Otherwise he remains under the curse. He must be redeemed or destroyed.

CHRIST BECAME ACCURSED FOR US

"Christ hath redeemed us from the curse of the law, being made a curse for us: for it is written, Cursed is every one that hangeth on a tree" (Gal. 3:13). This text enables us to understand the meaning of the following: "For their sakes I sanctify myself, that they also might be sanctified through the truth" (John 17:19).

We all know that Christ did not need to be purified from sin; for "he did no sin, neither was guile found in his mouth" (I Pet. 2:22). As our great High Priest he was "holy, harmless, undefiled, separate from sinners, and made higher than the heavens" (Heb. 7:26). When he sanctified himself it simply meant that he consecrated himself to go over on the accursed side of the book of judgment and be made accursed for us. In doing so he did not become actually alienated from God; for "every devoted [*cherem*, accursed] thing is most holy unto the Lord" (Lev. 27:28).

Christ seems here to set a special example for us. Born without sin and living without sin, he did not need to be converted. Yet he set us a pattern when as a child he made a profession of devotion to the Father's business (Luke 2:49). So far as he was concerned, he did not need to be baptized; and yet in order to "fulfill all righteousness" as an example to us he was baptized by John in the Jordan (Matt. 3:15). And although he never knew the stain of carnality, he set us an example by consecrating himself to death, as recorded in John 17.

HOLINESS AS MORAL PURITY

The study of the term holy in the Old Testament begins with its ceremonial meaning, its first application being to things, which, of course, have no moral quality. It was not long, however, until various persons were described as being holy because they belonged to God in some special sense. The priests of the sanctuary belonged to God—they were holy. But if even an unclean animal was unworthy of sacrifice on God's altar because of its uncleanness, it is far more apparent that a man or a people who belong to God must be like him in moral character. Before tracing the moral nature of holiness it is important to note that use of the word holy in a ceremonial sense extends to the New Testament itself. Jesus said that the temple sanctifies the gold (Matt. 23:17). This is, of course, a ceremonial use of the word, as no moral purity can be attached to gold. The saints at Corinth, both Jews and Gentiles, were thoroughly familiar with the idea that the Gentiles were unclean—ceremonially defiled—to the Jews. There the question arose: Should a Christian husband or wife live with an unclean, unbelieving, heathen companion? The Apostle Paul says yes; in Judaism the unclean thing defiled the clean, but in this case the unbelieving husband or wife is sanctified by the believing companion, "else were your children unclean; but now are they holy" (I Cor. 7:12-14). The unbelieving partner is ceremonially cleansed from his heathen defilement, and his part-heathen child also is not partaker of the heathen defilement. Both are ceremonially clean and not repugnant to the true Israel of God.

Of course, the Apostle is not preaching infant baptism, because, if the child of the heathen by being made ceremonially holy in this way was fit for baptism, by the same reasoning the unbelieving partner would also be fit for baptism; and this no theologian has ever maintained.

JUSTIFIED CHRISTIANS CEREMONIALLY HOLY

It will solve one of the biggest problems in the doctrine of sanctification if we clearly see the point that this same idea of ceremonial holiness was applied to all Christians from the moment of their conversion.

"As such were some of you: but ye are washed, but ye are sanctified, but ye are justified in the name of the Lord Jesus, and by the Spirit of our God" (I Cor. 6:11). This text has baffled holiness preachers for many generations; for the term sanctified is applied even before that of justification, and if a person is sanctified before he is justified critics are certainly warranted in questioning as to how he can be sanctified as a second work of grace after justification. The answer is very simple when we remember that all Christians are sanctified in the ceremonial sense that ancient Israel was a holy people. But in the same epistle the Apostle Paul pointed out the carnality in the hearts of these sanctified people, which proved that their sanctification was only formal and ceremonial and was by no means an entire sanctification of the nature in the complete enduement of moral purity.

THE HOLINESS OF GOD

Regarded from a historical standpoint, it is evident that the first conception which the people of Israel would form of the holiness of God would be that of *the supreme power which lays claim to a man's possession,* and later they understood that he *lays claim to the man himself.* At the beginning, God's holiness was interpreted to mean *his possessiveness;* throughout long ages of time the idea was gradually revealed that the man whom God *owned and controlled* ought to be *inwardly, morally, like God.*

But what was God like? Revelations of the moral quality of God's holiness undoubtedly came slowly, like the rising of the winter's sun; little by little the light stole into the hearts of men, revealing that *the holiness of God is his supreme moral excellence.* It is the perfect balance of a supreme excellence of all moral attributes, conceived not as a mere transitory whim but as an eternal faithfulness—a granite character of unchanging, moral perfection which, viewed from the standpoint of our world, projects itself as unchangeable and immovable will into all the future relations of God to his creatures.

Dr. William Newton Clarke has defined it is follows:

> Holiness is the glorious fullness of God's moral excellence, held as the principle of his own action and the standard for his creatures....
>
> Thus holiness is not God's character alone, or God's self-consistency alone, or God's requirement alone. It is all three. It is his character consistently acted out by himself and unalterably insisted upon with us men.[1]

HOLINESS IN HUMAN NATURE

We do not doubt that the moral image of God restored to the soul of a Christian endows that person with a finite and limited image, or copy, of the divine perfections in their moral aspects. But here it is important to realize that we are viewing the reflection of an infinite sun as it is seen in the finite, imperfect, or incomplete, in the weak and fallible mirror of human nature. Viewed in this imperfect mirror, what is the form holiness takes?

Now we are at the point where most of the mistakes regarding Christian perfection have arisen. If we think of a reflection of a perfect image of God, free from all distortions of ignorance, narrowness of mind, feebleness of reason, limita-

1. William Newton Clarke, *An Outline of Christian Theology*, pp. 89, 91.

tions of social customs and conditioning we shall form a false definition of holiness in human nature; for we shall expect the reproduction of the *very being* of the infinite God within finite humanity, instead of *a reproduction of his image.* We shall be attempting to define human nature as free from human limitations and superior to human finiteness. All of this is futile, and this is perhaps the point where Christian perfection has been most liable to misconception and abuse.

PERFECT LOVE

In his recent scholarly work on Christian perfection, Dr. W. E. Sangster emphasizes the inappropriateness of the term "Christian perfection." He thinks that the use of this term by the Wesleys was extremely unfortunate and that the expression "perfect love" would have been better from every standpoint. It would have been more scriptural, more philosophical, and likewise more acceptable to the general public. It would have relieved the doctrine of an unnecessary load of ridicule and misconception. Elsewhere, it has been pointed out that love is the fulfilling of the law.[2] And I feel constrained to describe the form which holiness takes in the Christian as being expressed by perfect love. In this conception we are not dealing with pharisaical conceptions of law and the philosophic tricks of moral casuistry. We drive the drill of reason and conscience through all the hard rocks of legalism into the pool of rich oil which lies in the heart of undivided love and devotion to God as revealed in Christ.

2. Cf. Charles E. Brown, *The Meaning of Salvation,* p. 70.

In this region we come into harmony with the popular thought and conscience of the whole world. Everywhere men really believe that "love is the fulfilling of the law;" and wherever it can be shown that man has acted with loyal and devoted sympathy and inward, personal attachment to the purposes of the law, all juries and all courts everywhere incline to be satisfied with the defense. The Scriptures teach that such an attitude satisfies God.

THE MEANING OF LOVE

Love to God by no means signifies sentimental attachment to certain ritual, dogma, theories, or outward religion in and of themselves; it is love for God as a person as revealed to us in Jesus Christ. Such love inspires the intellect with appreciation of, and devotion to, the principles of the beloved. It inspires the heart with the devotion to the nature of the character of God as the holy one, and it strengthens the will to cling to the Holy One with an unwavering devotion.

In this earthly life there is no higher conception of man's relation to God. The man who loves God with a pure heart completely will not sin, because this attitude of his heart constitutes the complete fulfillment of God's demands upon him. Fifteen hundred years ago Augustine wrote, "It is good that I should cling to God"; and Jovinian, a monk of the same era, taught, as summarized by Harnack: "In him who occupies this relationship of faith and love there is nothing to be condemned; he can commit no sin which would separate him from God."[3] This is the message of the Apostle John, who

3. Adolph Harnack, *History of Dogma,* Vol. V, p. 58.

wrote: "Herein is our love made perfect, that we may have boldness in the day of judgment: because as he is, so are we in this world" (I John 4:17).

Ceremonial, or objective, holiness, then, is ownership by God. Subjective, or moral, holiness, however, is a love infused into our hearts by the supernatural work of the Holy Spirit and by that same Spirit made perfect, or complete.

IS ENTIRE SANCTIFICATION A GIFT OR AN ATTAINMENT?

The church of the New Testament age understood very well that all the miracles of God's redemptive power must always be accepted upon the level of grace; in other words, they are gifts. When Paul insists so strenuously upon justification by faith he does so to emphasize the fact that salvation is a gift from God and nothing which anybody can do is sufficient to earn that blessing. But in the course of the weary ages of apostasy the idea grew up that such a way of salvation was too simple and too easy—and we might also add, too infrequent. And so the idea gained ground in the ancient Catholic church that God does indeed give salvation, but he gives it only at the end of a long process of laborious striving and good works, which must precede salvation and make the recipient worthy of the gift. Or we might say, salvation is given to those who by a lifetime of laborious and ascetic works have proved themselves worthy of receiving it. In this way the idea grew up that all of life is to be employed as a preparation for salvation in the future life. The rarest saints receive this gift of salvation sometime in this mortal life. Others receive it at the moment of death, but most people must continue the process of preparation for salvation by an indefinite period of pain and suffering in purgatory before they are good enough to receive justification and salvation.

Martin Luther was able to see through this fallacy of reasoning. He argued that if justification is a gift and not a payment of wages, then there is nothing a man can do to make himself worthy of it except simply to put himself in a receptive attitude of faith. Thus Luther reasoned justly concerning justification, but neither he nor any prominent leader of that age was able to apply the same logic to the experience of entire sanctification. Here they employed the identical type of reasoning which had been used in the Catholic church to prove that justification was an experience usually attainable in the future life. How completely the form of theology followed the traditional pattern of Catholic dogma is shown in the following quotation from the *Westminster Confession of Faith:*

> The bodies of men, after death, return to dust, and see corruption; but their souls (which neither die nor sleep), having an immortal subsistence, immediately return to God who gave them. The souls of the righ teous, being then made perfect in holiness, are received into the highest heavens, where they behold the face of God in light and glory.[4]

As I have previously shown, these foundation Protestant creeds had held firmly and earnestly to the view that there is a sinful nature remaining in the regenerate, a nature which

4. *The Westminster Confession of Faith* (1647), XXXH, Art. 1.

Wesleyan theologians call inbred sin. And now we read in the greatest of these creeds of English-speaking Protestantism that this inbred sin may not be removed until the end of life. Many trained theologians can see that the obscurity here is a complete reflection of the obscurity of Catholic theology regarding justification—exactly at the same point. I might suggest that the mystery is made a little deeper because Protestant theologians did not dare to suggest that inbred sin is removed in any purgatory after death. The suggestion is that it is removed in the instant of dying, and most thoughtful people would be inclined to think that if this is so there must be something in the very nature of human flesh which makes holiness in this life impossible. To admit this is to turn back to Manicheism, one of the most ancient and dangerous heresies of the church, and hold that sin is an inherent part of human nature on its physical side. In other words, that would amount to denying the holiness of the human body of Christ or that he had come in a holy, human body. Because there is no human thought sharp enough to penetrate such theological contradiction the point is left obscure in order that each may draw his own conclusion.

The distinction between gift and attainment is not too difficult for presentation in popular thought. A certain child is gifted in music, but after years of training he is thought to be able to give a much finer performance than was possible at the beginning of his career. On the other hand, a person with no musical talent, if such a person were imaginable, could not make improvement. Our illustration is difficult because perhaps every normal being has at least a slight musical gift. Think of a human eye. A normal human eye has a gift of sight, and yet that gift may be trained to exceptional skill with a microscope, in distinguishing color, or otherwise in finding obscure things which others cannot see. But it is entirely based upon the gift of sight, without which skill is impossible.

And so we grant there is attainment of skill in the pursuit of holiness. That is the experience which Christians call growth in grace. It represents an increase of sensitivity, a sharpening of conscience, and a strengthening of judgment, such as belong to those "that are of full age, even those who by reason of use have their senses exercised to discern both good and evil" (Heb. 5:14). It also represents an increase of skill and ability in doing the work of the Lord, and all this is accompanied by an increasing strength of resolution by which the soul gradually settles into that final state of unchangeable devotion to God which will mark the end of probation.

If we are willing to accept the doctrine of entire sanctification in conformity with the fundamental idea of all Protestant theology and the essential teaching of the New Testament, we come to the view that entire sanctification is the completion of the work of redemption, and as such it must be a gift. At this point we dare not take the road of Roman Catholic tradition and hold regarding sanctification as they have done regarding justification—that sanctification is the reward of a good life. It is contrary to the essential principles of Protestant theology to believe thus of any phase of the work of redemption. No fruit of the atoning passion of Christ can be reached by means of good works. Not so can we reach justification. Neither can we reach entire sanctification by that road. Entire sanctification comes to us as the result of the atoning passion of Christ. (See Hebrews 13:12.) No definition of sanctification is pressed here. It is urged, rather, that any kind of sanctification must be a kind purchased by the death of Christ without the gate; and as such it is not the reward of works, not the product of discipline and growth, but a gift accepted by faith.

Here we note another Catholic tradition not fully deserted by Protestant theology. In the New Testament, the grace of God is God's merciful, unmerited favor, his personal disposition of favor toward us; whereas in Catholic theology grace has been objectified in some kind of concrete thing standing alone in its own light and mediated to us through the sacraments. Protestant theology has inherited this Catholic conception of grace by conceiving sanctification as a gradual growth in grace. The grace here seems to be some kind of thing separate from God, which gradually accumulates in the soul until approximate sanctification is attained by all and marks the end of such a process. But grace is never a thing. Grace is God's personal attitude toward us and it is always a gift; it is never earned.

The trend of this discussion throughout has tended to develop the thesis that entire sanctification is a gift accepted by faith. It may occur any time that faith mounts the hill of promise, where its belief becomes sight and is melted into knowledge.

XI.
HOW IS ENTIRE SANCTIFICATION RECEIVED?

For two hundred years Wesleyan theologians have taught with almost monotonous unanimity that entire sanctification is received through consecration and faith. This is the true and correct formula, by which millions of people have swept into the glory of an experience that made life stronger, more victorious, and more joyful than they had ever before imagined possible. Nevertheless, use has worn these words to a point where for many they no longer embody clearcut and definite ideas. My purpose here is not to deny or to change these great principles, but to expound them in order to reveal their true meaning.

ARE THERE TWO CONDITIONS?

First of all we must ask, Are there two conditions or just one condition? Is the true formula consecration and faith, or faith and consecration? Or, in conformity with the Protestant theory of justification, should we merely say faith alone? Wesley was hostile to any limitation of the conditions of justification or sanctification to faith alone. He regarded such a formula as conducive to antinomianism (moral anarchy). He thought it tended to make people neglect their duty and imagine that their thinking would save them. It must be admitted that this is a real difficulty; nevertheless, I would hold with Luther, even against Wesley, that faith alone is the sole condition of salvation and of entire sanctification. This expression makes sense and agrees completely with the language of Paul. This fact endears the expression to us even though it should be liable to misunderstanding and abuse.

As has been previously pointed out,[1] faith for salvation includes repentance as one of its component elements, without which it cannot be saving faith. And this is the way we must interpret faith for entire sanctification. Such faith must include perfect consecration as an integral part of its nature, and this seems reasonable and right. There can be no consecration without faith; there can be no vital faith without consecration in this area of the Christian life. Anybody who has been through high school should understand that such colors as green and red are component elements of the nature of white light. Wherever there is white light, there is green light and red light among the other colors of the spectrum. Like-

1. Charles E. Brown, *The Meaning of Salvation*, p. 97.

wise, there must be consecration and faith combined together in the heart that seeks the glory of entire sanctification.

Nevertheless, for clearness of thought it is necessary for us to separate these two elements in order to give each its proper treatment. And perhaps here it is better to follow the time-honored formula—consecration and faith. Our prism of doctrine separates the rays for further study.

CONSECRATION FOR ENTIRE SANCTIFICATION

At this point, the earnest student of the subject finds himself confronted with many baffling difficulties. First of all, the Modern English New Testaments nearly always translate the Greek word *hagiazo*, or sanctify (make holy), by the English word "consecrate." Young people, finding the word shuffled before their eyes in the manner of a slight-of-hand performer, are baffled utterly; for in common church usage the word "consecrate" is taken to mean what a person does for himself and "sanctify" refers to what God does for a person. There is no question that these translations have misled millions of people into thinking that the New Testament teaches sanctification to be a process of endless repetition of a never-completed consecration of the Christian believer.

If it were the intention of the translators to concoct a doctrine of sanctification that, after all, is the old, traditional Catholic doctrine, then they have taken very effective means of doing so. In this case they are guilty of wresting the Word of God, because a large portion of these texts refer to what God does for a person and are not suspectible of such an interpretation. In this connection we must remember that the

Greek word has never been changed; and that word, commonly translated "sanctify" in the Authorized Version, is the Greek word *hagiazo,* which means "to make holy."

No scholarship can change this fundamental fact, as it is not the business of scholars to change facts but to discover them and explain their relations. However, "consecrate" can be used as practically a synonym of "sanctify." They are both derived from Latin words and may be understood to mean the same thing. To think of them in this way is the simplest way to read the New Testament in modern English. Nevertheless, in this connection, I shall use the word consecrate as signifying the dedication which a person makes of himself to God and the term sanctify to indicate that work which God, by his Spirit, performs in the soul.

HOW SHALL THE HOLY BE SANCTIFIED?

The next difficulty which meets the casual reader is that in numerous instances throughout the New Testament even justified Christians are called holy. The church is composed of all Christians, and the church is holy. How can we consecrate to God that which is already his and how can that be sanctified which is already holy? These points have already been discussed briefly elsewhere. The old Wesleyan theologians taught that sanctification begins in conversion. The second crisis experience is the reception of *entire sanctification.* I have shown also that in our common thought we make a distinction between the private possessions of a man—such as his watch and shoes—and his general possessions, such as the grass that grows on his lawn. This is a valid distinction because it is rooted in our common experiences of life. One cannot deny that all Christians do belong to God and that all Christians are holy in a sense, but I have tried to show that all Christians are holy partly in a ceremonial or objective sense, not entirely in the experience of moral purity. Moreover, our common experiences indicate that sinners who come to God have no call to consecration and no conception of it as a general rule. They come surrendering as persons seeking mercy and not as friends offering service.

Here we must return to the greatest paradox in religion. Augustine said, "I would not have sought thee, had I not found thee." In other words, no man would ever seek for God unless there were some revelation of the divine beauty to lure his soul onward in its zealous quest. Elsewhere reference has been made to sanctification as an act of man giving his assent and conforming his will to that holiness of God which he cannot increase or diminish but which he might insult by ignoring. The Christian believer undertakes the work of entire consecration because he would confirm by the deep consent of his own will that ownership of God which is already implicit in his acceptance as a Christian.

Similar experiences of human life are too numerous to mention. Millions of men have found themselves actually in conditions more or less similar to, or even contrary to, what they had expected. Then by an act of the will they have mentally adjusted themselves to the new condition which was already a fact. People move into a new home in a faraway country. They came there through their own will, but as they settle down they find conditions they never anticipated. Sometimes they perform an act of will by which they gradually and slowly adjust themselves to the new surroundings and live there afterwards in peace. Many married people mentally adjust themselves to marriages months and sometimes years after the objective adjustment has been made. These are legitimate figures of the adjustment of consecration which the justified believer makes to an objective experience entered into at the time when he was saved and this consecration is of that which already belongs to God objectively.

This use of the words "sanctify" and "consecrate" is not tortured out of a theological state of mind but is drawn from the Word of God: "Sanctify unto me all the first born…it is mine" (Exod. 13:2). One can easily see that in the strictest sense it is impossible to give anything to God; for our lives, and all the earth, and nature belong to him. Consecration of the Christian is accomplished by a deep, heartfelt recognition of the fact that he belongs to God and by rights ought to belong to God; it is a heart adjustment of his will to that way of life. Nonetheless, it is the solemn duty of the justified believer to make this solemn dedication and consecration of himself to God. "I beseech you therefore, brethren, by the mercies of God, that ye present your bodies a living sacrifice, holy, acceptable unto God, which is your reasonable service" (Rom. 12:1).

Against this monumental New Testament text (Rom. 12:1) pointing definitely to a crisis experience in the life of a Christian there has been directed for generations the constantly weakening effect of the Catholic tradition. That tradition tends to melt the definite into the indefinite, the certain into the uncertain. It makes the one positive, irrevocable dedication melt into a million pious prayers of consecration to be repeated over and over again. Against the sharp, clear-cut, definite experience of the death of an animal stricken at the altar in an act never to be repeated, this tradition brings a fallacious theory of "dying daily." What the Apostle meant by "dying daily" was not that he died to sin daily, but that he daily faced the danger of physical death, in the actual realization of his once-for-all consecration to Christ on the altar. This dissolving, repetitious theory of consecration is one of the most dangerous features of our present-day religious life, because after it has destroyed and cut away like acid the clear-cut doctrine of sanctification as a definite once-for-all consecration to God, it will continue to destroy the definite experience of conversion and the witness of the Spirit to salvation. It covers the whole Christian life with a fog of uncertainty and makes every text of the Bible a mere approximation which might mean anything.

PRESENT YOUR BODIES

One of the most disastrous consequences of the entrance of the world of sinners into the historical church and the acceptance of the life of sin as the normal Christian life has been this cloud of defeat and discouragement which has thereby been thrown over multitudes of professed Christians. This defeatism has become a tradition in historical Christianity, being manifested in one respect by a continuous repetition of confession of sin and prayers for forgiveness. Millions of Christians consider that no prayer is acceptable to God unless it contains both these elements; whereas the fact is that a confession of sin which a person does not sincerely realize is a sin in itself. This repetition has permeated the whole religious life of a vast section of Christendom. People pray repeatedly thousands of times for forgiveness without ever being conscious of sin or sure of forgiveness. This same tradition of repetition has recently sought to force itself upon the interpretation of the text in Romans 12:1: "I beseech you, therefore, brethren, by the mercies of God, that ye present your bodies a living sacrifice, holy, acceptable unto God, which is your reasonable service." We are told that this consecration is an act of worship which is to be repeated over and over ten thousand times, just as often as we have occasion to remember it. This conclusion is drawn from the fact that this consecration is said to be "your reasonable service," which might be translated "your rational or spiritual worship." The Greek word here is *latreia,* which originally meant "to serve for hire"; as a noun it is translated "service" everywhere in the New Testament. The verb is generally translated "to serve," although it is rendered "worship" in four places. In the present text the reference is not to occasionally interrupted and repeated acts of worship, but to the continuous ritual of the Temple. This ritual did not consist of occasional or seasonal ceremonies, like the convening of modern assemblies, but was carried on continuously from age to age, as long as the Temple stood.

In the spiritual temple, of which the earthly Temple was a type, all Christians are priests: "And hath made us kings and priests unto God and his Father" (Rev. 1:6); "Ye…are… an holy priesthood" (I Pet. 2:5); "A royal priesthood" (vs. 9).

These priests do not merely visit the spiritual temple occasionally; they "serve him day and night in his temple" (Rev. 7:15). In other words, the worship of the Christian is not merely something he takes up once a week or once a month; it is a continuous service of his life. He worships God in spirit and in truth continually, not occasionally. Paul expressed it "instantly serving [*latreuog*] God day and night" (Acts 26:7).

Now the noblest duty, the most important act, of the priest is to offer himself, that is, present his body; and the verb used here is in the aorist tense, which indicates an act which is completed at one time. The same language is used in Romans 6:13 where Christians are exhorted to "yield yourselves unto God, as those who are alive from the dead, and your members as instruments of righteousness unto God." Here the aorist tense indicates completed life and death consecration. The verb here is the same as the one translated "present" in Romans 12:1. And the meaning of the tense is very beautifully brought out if we observe that the *yielding to unrighteousness* is in the *present* tense and the *yielding to God* in the *aorist* tense, so that we might read: "Neither repeatedly yield ye your members as instruments of unrighteousness unto sin; but once for all yield yourselves unto God as those that are alive from the dead." In other words, most people keep on repeating their acts of sin even though they express a desire for reformation. This course Paul forbids and commands a once-for-all, life-and-death consecration. We notice the same idea in I Peter 2:5, where "to offer up spiritual sacrifices" is in the aorist and signifies sacrifices made once for all. However, there are sacrifices which the Christian offers repeatedly, for example, "the sacrifice of praise" (Heb. 13:15). There the verb is in the present tense. We are commanded: "To do good and to communicate forget not" (vs. 16). "Forget not" is in the present tense, indicating continuous repetition. Likewise the "well pleased" of the Father. Support of this interpretation is found in the opinion of Dean Henry Alford, formerly dean of Canterbury and a famous commentator, who writes on I Peter 2:5: "...to offer up (no habitual offering, as in rite or festival, is meant, but the one, once-for-all, devotion of the body, as in Romans 12:1, to God as His)."[2]

DANGERS OF REPEATING CONSECRATION

Repetition of consecration is quite fashionable today. There is a popular idea that consecration can be made stronger by constantly repeating it, but that idea is open to question. Do we believe in a man's truthfulness any more on account of his repetitious claim to be telling the truth? Does not the repetition sometimes awaken doubt? Peter repeated the assertion that he did not know Christ and finally tried to make it more secure by an oath, but repetition did not make his story true. Christ's standard is: Let your Yea be yea, and your Nay, nay. That is also the standard of wise men everywhere. Does anyone believe that people are strengthened and made better by going through an ordeal of making and breaking a set of New Year's resolutions each year? Do you have any less confidence in the people who consistently live right by habitual inclination? The vows of consecration are like the vows of marriage, and do we really think that anything could

2. Henry Alford, *The New Testament for English Readers,* Vol. IV, p. 800.

be gained by repeating the marriage vows every few months? Most of us have known people who divorced and re-married each other repeatedly, but we never thought that that was the mark of a successful or happy married life. Constant making and breaking of habits is detrimental to the formation of a strong will, and a continuous repetition of the vows of consecration is likely to unsettle a person in his Christian experience and dim the witness of the Spirit in his heart. The work of Christ is final: "For by one offering he hath perfected forever them that are sanctified" (Heb. 10:14); "This is the will of God even your sanctification" (I Thess. 4:3). "By the which will we are sanctified through the offering of the body of Jesus Christ once for all" (Heb. 10:10).

Similar in spirit, though different in words, is the following exhortation of Paul: "Having therefore these promises, dearly beloved, let us cleanse ourselves from all filthiness of the flesh and spirit, perfecting holiness in the fear of God" (II Cor. 7:1). Here, too, we only spoil the meaning when we cover it up with the fog of uncertainty and repetitiousness. This is a definite act which Christians are to do, in which they denounce the carnal mind and consecrate themselves for the experience of entire sanctification. The "filthiness of the flesh and spirit" here reminds us of the "superfluity of naughtiness" in James 1:21, which even a truly great scholar, Theodore Zahn does not hesitate to translate "residue—remainder," following Mark 8:8. He adds: "The writer means the old, hereditary faults which still cling even to those born of God."[3]

3. Theodore Zahn, *Introduction to the New Testament,* Vol. I, p. 96.

Fresh light on the meaning of consecration may be drawn from the Hebrew word translated consecrate in the Authorized Version. The renderings of these are as follows: (1) to devote (used once); (2) to separate (used three times); (3) to set apart (used seven times); (4) to fill the hand (used eighteen times); (5) filling up (used eleven times).

The expression "to fill the hand," used so often in the Hebrew of the Old Testament and translated consecrate in the Authorized Version, is a reference to the custom of placing a sacrificial offering in the hands of the new priest, to symbolize his authority to offer sacrifices and his consecration to the work of the priesthood. This suggests to us that the Holy Spirit must give the seeker for entire sanctification the spiritual conception that he has something to offer. In other words, it is the Spirit who consecrates him by giving him the consciousness that there is an offering in his hand. This word is also a suggestion of the two sides of sanctification: the consecration which the individual makes in the dedication of himself; and the enduement of power and the investment with authority which God gives at the same instant, honoring the consecrated priest with the fullness of his priestly authority and spiritual power.

The man who thinks that his hands are empty is naturally not prepared to make the consecration. He needs to tarry in prayer until he reaches the point when this consecration becomes a reality in his experience and a definite crisis in his life. Consecration is the answer which love makes to God's claims of a complete personal ownership and devotion. This love, of course, is the "love of God…shed abroad in our hearts by the Holy Ghost" (Rom. 5:5), without which no real Christian life can ever exist. "What doth the Lord thy God require of thee, but to fear the Lord thy God, to walk in all his ways, and to love him, and to serve the Lord thy God with all thy heart and with all thy soul" (Deut. 10:12).

I. The commandment of the entire Scriptures, from beginning to end, is that of perfect consecration to God; and the spring and energy of that consecration is love.

1. The love of God is the same in the Old Testament and in the New. It is not a sentiment of the mind alone, nor an affection of the sensibility alone, nor an energy of the will alone; but it is the devotion of the man, in the integrity of all these, to God as the one Object and Rest and Center and Life of the soul. "What doth the Lord thy God require of thee, but to fear the Lord thy God, to walk in all his ways, and to love him, and to serve the Lord thy God with all thy heart and with all thy soul?" (Deut. 10:12). Here perfect love stands between perfect fear and perfect service as the bond and complement of both. Our Lord has not even changed the words, which he quotes; he has not said of this: "A new commandment I give unto you" (John 13:34). It is the old commandment which ye had from the beginning, the universal law of all intelligent creatures: to make God their only Object, the Supreme End of their existence; the neighbor and all other things being objects of love only in him, hid with Christ in God. This command-

ment is the measure of evangelical privilege, which the believer has only to accept, and wonder at, and believe, and attain.

2. Its perfection is simply its soleness and supremacy. It is not in the measure of its intensity, which never ceases to increase throughout eternity until it reaches the maximum, if such there be, of creaturely strength; but, in the quality of its unique and sovereign ascendancy, it has the crisis of perfection set before it as attainable. In the interpretation of heaven that love is perfect which carries with it the whole man and all that he has and is. Its perfection is negative, when no other object, that is no creature, receives it apart from God or in comparison of him; and it is positive when the utmost strength of the faculties, in the measure and according to the degree of their possibility on earth, is set on him. Thus interpreted no law of the Bible is more absolute than this of the perfect love of God. "Thou shalt love the Lord thy God with all thy heart, and with all thy soul, and with all thy strength, and with all thy mind" (Luke 10:27). Omitting the last, "with all thy mind," this was the ancient law, concerning which the promise was: "The Lord thy God will circumcise thine heart, and the heart of thy seed, to love the Lord thy God" (Deut. 30:6). The quaternion of attributes—or the heart as the one personality, to which the understanding and affections and will belong—as our Lord has completed it, leaves no room for imperfection. However far this

may go beyond our theories and our hopes and our attainments, it is and must be the standard of privilege. We are now concerned only with the privileges of the covenant of redemption as administered by the Holy Ghost.

II. The Spirit of God, as the Spirit of perfect consecration, is poured out upon the Christian church. And he discharges his sanctifying office as an indwelling Spirit: able perfectly to fill the soul with love, and to awaken perfect love in return.

1. The last document of the New Testament gives clear expression to the former. We love [him] because he first loved us. The Divine love to man in redemption is revealed to the soul for its conversion; and it is shed abroad in the regenerate spirit as the mightiest argument of its gratitude. "We have known and believed the love that God hath to us" (I John 4:16): this revelation received by faith was the secret of our return to God. But John again and again speaks of this love as perfected in us: that is, as accomplishing its perfect triumph over the sin and selfishness of our nature, and its separation from God, which is the secret of all sin and self. "In him verily is the love of God perfected" (2:5): this ensures its being individual, and contains the very utmost for which we plead. The love of God, as his mightiest instrument for the sanctification of the spirit of man, is declared to have in him its perfect work. The "verily" rebukes our unbelief and encourages our hope.

2. He also speaks most expressly of the return of love to God in us as perfected. This expression occurs but once in the Scripture in so absolutely incontestable a form. Whereas in the previous instances the Apostle meant that the love of God is perfected in us, in the following words he can have no other meaning than that our own love is to be, and is—for these are the same, in our argument—itself perfected. It is of course the same thing whether God's love is perfected or ours made perfect in return; but the combination gives much force to the statement of privilege: "Perfect love casteth out fear....He that feareth is not made perfect in love" (I John 4:18). As John is the only writer who says that God is love, so he is the only one who speaks of a Christian's perfect love. This solitary text, however, gives its meaning to a multitude. It is the last testimony that glorifies all that has gone before.
3. The Holy Ghost uses the love of God as his instrument in effecting an entire consecration. This is that unction from the Holy One which makes us all partakers of the Savior's consecration, Who received the Spirit not by measure for us. As the Supreme Christ was perfectly consecrated in the love of God and man, so it is the privilege of every Christian, who is by his name an image of Christ, to be perfectly consecrated. And there is no limitation of the Spirit's office in the reproduction of the Christly character in us. This was the lesson of that great and notable day of the

Lord, the Pentecost. On the morning of that day the Spirit's elect symbol was fire. First he appeared as the Shekinah glory, without a veil, diffused over the whole Church, and then resting upon each. The light which touched every forehead for acceptance entered as fire each heart, "and they were all filled with the Holy Ghost" (Acts 2:2-4): filled literally for the time being; and, if we suppose that indwelling permanent, we have our doctrine substantiated. That in this there may be continuance we are taught by Paul: "Be filled with the Spirit" (Eph. 5:18). Lastly, as a tongue, the symbol signified the sanctification of the outward life of devotion to God and service to man. Hence there is no limit to the Spirit's consecrating grace. "I sanctify myself, that they also might be sanctified" (John 17:19). This is the Savior's example where it is perfectly imitable: the methods of our sanctification, and its process in the destruction of alien affections, find no pattern in him; but the result shines clearly in his example. "Beholding as in a glass the glory of the Lord, [we] are changed into the same image from glory to glory, even as by the Spirit of the Lord" (II Cor. 3:18). We receive unto perfection the glory which we reflect.[4]

THE PROBLEM OF RECONSECRATION

If a finite creature like man can be possessed of an infinite hunger and unmeasured yearning, then the human heart cer-

4. William Burt Pope, *A Compendium of Christian Theology*, pp. 51-53.

tainly possesses such a yearning for God, and undoubtedly the deepest saint would not dare to spurn the opportunity to pray for more of God. If a public call is made, asking: "Who desires to get nearer to God, to become more spiritual, to live closer to God?" undoubtedly it will be the most spiritual and the most deeply consecrated who will respond to such a call. This fact has made appeals to reconsecration very popular among us, and the response to such appeals is usually so satisfactory that no afterthought is ever given to the significance of such an appeal. But I believe that the whole subject deserves more consideration in the light of the doctrine of entire sanctification.

We often hear it said that there are unconsecrated areas in the life of every Christian, and it is his business to consecrate these areas as he discovers them. To say the least, this is an unfortunate way of expressing whatever truth there is in the theory, because it is, in form at least, a complete surrender of the doctrine of entire sanctification as a crisis experience, once for all, in human life. This theory of unconsecrated areas of life is simply a statement of the doctrine of gradual sanctification, and is fully consistent with such a theory. If the unexplored regions of life are therefore unconsecrated, it is simply impossible for any man to be wholly consecrated at any time before the moment of his death, because who knows what regions of life lie around him as yet unexplored.

The doctrine of entire sanctification teaches that when the center and core of a man's heart is consecrated, then all of these outlying regions are likewise consecrated, too. When a Christian sets up the flag of Immanuel on the continent of his soul he means that all the areas of that continent belong to the King Immanuel, whether he ever makes an intellectual discovery of them or not.

Sometimes a theory of reconsecration may cover a false view of a Christian's mission in life. It is possible, for example, to think of a Christian duty to master every possible phase of living and fill it with success. This, however, is a false view of the meaning of life, as a little reflection will show anyone. It is the work of Christian asceticism to give up the good things of life in order that the best may thereby be cultivated. We cut off a dozen good roses in order that the best rose may flower to its finest development. This is a commonplace of natural life. A boy destroys his possibilities to be a doctor, a musician, a lawyer, or a skilled mechanic in order to be an expert accountant. He actually sacrifices all these other possibilities in order to realize this one which he prizes most. The idea of the Christian life is not to be a Jack-of-all-trades, but to be a master of one, a specialist in some spiritual realm of divine service. At least such a spiritual specialism is just as worthy as an attempt to develop all the possibilities of life. A Christian young man gives up, let us say, the possibility of developing his talents in any one of a dozen different ways in America in order to give all his strength to the development of his talent as a missionary in foreign lands. St. Francis of Assisi was, according to the record, a marvelous saint but he had no experience in life as husband and father, or in the joyful fellowship of a Christian in a modern evangelical church.

How a consecrated man should regard these areas of life, these potential personalities, which he has no call or duty to develop in himself, is well stated by a modern theologian, Dr. Leonard Hodgson, Regius Professor of Divinity in Oxford University. He writes:

> We are finite. Life is not long enough for each of us to give full expression to all his many selves. The love which is to unify them has therefore to take the form of recognizing the value of those which cannot be indulged. They are not to be suppressed or repressed as evil; they are to be offered in willing surrender to God because He wills us to give precedence to some other self as the center of the particular work that he has for us to do on earth. The man who is called to be a scholar must curb his desire to engage in manifold practical activities. If for a while he has to go and be a soldier, he must put aside his civilian pursuits. If he is called to work in which marriage is impossible, he must be continent with a good grace. But he will only do any of these things with a good grace if he maintains a gracious attitude towards the selves he cannot satisfy, if he avoids the temptation to seal up the doors of his mind against the interests he cannot pursue and lets a love for them fertilize and enrich, without distracting, the self which is to be the center of his life.
>
> This graciousness cannot be achieved by man except by the grace of God. Our natural pride makes us disinclined to acknowledge that we are finite beings who cannot foster all kinds of good; it inclines us to justify our self-limitation by holding that we have chosen what is better and renounced what is worse. So long as

> we are trusting in our own strength, our natural weakness requires us to buttress our self-denial by building up a sentiment of reprobation or scorn towards the interests we have renounced. Thus the achievement of a false unity in our own lives makes us incapable of taking a further step in graciousness, and appreciating the contributions which others can make to human life, just because they are different from our own. It may be they are called to put in the center selves which we have to put on one side. It may be that they can express selves which we do not seem to have in us at all, which may indeed even be uncongenial to our tastes.[5]

Let us suppose that a young Christian discovers an area of life in which he feels it is his duty to work, and yet he finds himself unequal to his responsibility. Here the proper method is not to reconsecrate, but to reaffirm his consecration, and then begin the slow and sometimes tedious task of acquiring spiritual skill in the realm of Christian life where he would labor. A young man consecrates himself, let us say, to be an artist, but he finds that his hands are unskilled. The pictures he draws are crude. He does not need to consecrate again, but he needs to devote himself, to train his hands, until the vision of beauty in his brain gradually masters the clumsiness of his hands and the skill of his hands comes to match the vision of his heart.

And so it is in making new and fresh advances in hitherto unexplored fields of Christian living.

5. Leonard Hodgson, *The Doctrine of the Trinity*, pp. 185-186. Used by permission of Charles Scribner's Sons.

THE FUNDAMENTAL DECISION CALLS FOR MANY SMALLER DECISIONS

This fact probably expresses the truth in our frequent reiteration of the term "reconsecration." In his able exposition of the thought of Sören Kierkegaard, Dr. Eduard Geismar writes as follows:

> When the eternal is to be realized in time, it gives rise to the moment of decision, that crucial moment with its individual responsibility. And every decision just because it is a decision and because as such it confronts the future, involves the assumption of a risk. In his basic emphasis upon the risk, Kierkegaard would agree with William James. The moment of decision faces the future with its uncertainty; once made, the decision alters the personality. *After* the decision he is not the same man as he was *before* the decision. It is impossible so to safeguard this transition as to eliminate the sense of risk; every calculation of probability is impotent for this purpose, and can serve only to emasculate the decision. We see that subjectivity is a confrontation of the future in uncertainty and risk; this risk and this uncertainty evokes passion; the decision, when normally made, issues in a new determination of the self, and gives a distinctive content to the "moment."[6]

6. Eduard Geismar, *Lectures on the Religious Thought of Sören Kierkegaard*, pp. 46-47. Used by permission of Augsburg Publishing House.

I admit it is possible to call these constant minor decisions of the Christian life by the name of consecration or reconsecration. Under such a view a man is obligated to reconsecrate possibly several times a day, but I insist that it is just as logical to call these minor decisions conversions as it is to call them consecrations. The point is that the original consecration was a dedication of the self which commits a Christian to make every one of these decisions, each in its turn, as he comes to them just as the original vows of marriage bind a conscientious man or woman to repeated acts of devotion and fidelity to the companion in marriage.

Here is an illustration. A young man volunteers to serve in the Army. Some months later he finds himself on board a landing craft under command to leap out into the water in a hail of bullets. It is true that he will have to make a new decision, but he certainly will not have to join the Army again. The last decision he makes is simply an accessory to the original decision, which he made when he joined the Army. So I maintain that the smaller decisions of the Christian life are auxiliary to the one essential act of consecration which the believer made when he entered the experience of entire sanctification.

Nevertheless, these fresh new decisions of sacrificial devotion are not only inevitable if a man is to maintain his Christian integrity, but they are also very necessary, as Kierkegaard has indicated, in order to put fire and passion into the Christian experience. I am persuaded that any Christian life will be enthusiastic which daily faces up to the challenge of the cross, and constantly brings itself face to face with the risk and the danger of sacrificial decision for Christ in the constant everyday business of living the Christian life.

The danger of constant, formal reconsecration is that such a practice can create doubt as to the certainty of the consecration previously made. It infects the religious life with the repetitiousness of modern traditional religion and tends to create a doubt of the definite reality of our covenant relation with God.

I am ready at any time to join with other Christians in reaffirming my consecration, in restudying its implications, and in praying for a fresh outpouring of the spirit of holiness and power, but I cannot reconsecrate that to God which has already been consecrated to him, that which I have not withdrawn from his hands previously.

FORMS OF CONSECRATION

While I have never favored written prayers or anything of a mechanical nature in religion, it is possible that some people may derive benefit from the suggestions which they receive from reading well-written prayers or vows of consecration. These might have value by putting into definite words the inarticulate thoughts of the heart. In no case do I recommend them for mere mechanical memorization and repetition. First, here is the form of consecration written and signed by D. S. Warner, on December 13, 1877, although it is important to remember that he had already professed the experience of entire sanctification on June 6, 1877. What is given here is simply his attempt to give in itemized form the solemn covenant that constituted his consecration to God. He writes:

A covenant is an agreement of two parties in which both voluntarily bind themselves to fulfill certain conditions and receive certain benefits. God is the party of the first part of the contract, and has bound himself.

1. "I will put my laws into their minds and write them in their hearts."
2. "And I will be their God."
3. They "shall know me from the least to the greatest."
4. "I will be merciful to their unrighteousness."
5. "Their sins and their iniquities will I remember no more."

Oh, thou Most High God, thou hast left this covenant in thy Holy Book, saying, "If any man will take hold of my covenant."

Now, therefore, in holy fear and reverence I present myself as the party of the second part and subscribe my name to the holy article of agreement, and following thy example will here and now write down the conditions on my part.

"They shall be my people" (Jer. 31:33). Amen, Lord, I am thine forever.

The vow is passed beyond repeal;
Now will I set the solemn seal.

Lord, thou hast been true to thy covenant, though I have been most unfaithful and am now altogether unworthy to take hold of thy most gracious covenant.

But knowing that thou hast bound thyself in thy own free offer to "be merciful to their unrighteousness," I take courage to approach thee and would most earnestly beseech thee to fulfill thy wonderful offer to BE MY GOD; and I do most joyfully yield myself entirely TO BE THINE.

Therefore this soul which thou hast made in thine own image is placed wholly in thy hands to do with as seemeth good.

This mind shall think only for thy glory and the promotion of thy cause.

This will is thy will, O God!

The spirit within this body is now thine; do with it as thou wilt, in life and death.

This body is thy temple forevermore.

These hands shall work only for thee.

These eyes to see thy adorable works and thy holy law.

This tongue and these lips to speak only holiness unto the Lord.

These ears to hear thy voice alone.

These feet to walk only in thy ways.

And all my being is now and forever thine.

In signing my name to this solemn covenant I am aware that I bind myself to live, act, speak, think, move, sit, stand up, lie down, eat, drink, hear, see, feel, and whatsoever I do all the days and nights of my life to do all continually and exclusively to the glory of God. I must henceforth wear nothing but what honors

God. I must have nothing in my possession or under my control but such as I can consistently write upon, "Holiness unto the Lord." The place where I live must be wholly dedicated to God. Every item of goods or property that is under my control is hereby conveyed fully over into the hands of God to be used by him as he will and to be taken from my stewardship whenever the great Owner wishes, and it is not my business at all.

She whom I call my wife belongs forevermore to God. Use her as thou wilt and where thou wilt, and leave her with me, or take her from me, just as seemeth good to thee and to thy glory. Amen. Levilla Modest, whom we love as a dear child bestowed upon us by thy infinite goodness, is hereby returned to thee. If thou wilt leave us to care for her and teach her of her true Father and Owner, we will do the best we can by thy aid to make her profitable unto thee. But if thou deemest us unfit to rear her properly or wouldst have her in thy more immediate presence, behold, she is thine, take her. Amen and Amen.

And now, great and merciful Father, thou to whom I belong, with all that pertains to me, and thou who art mine with all that pertains to thy fullness and richness, all this offering which I have made would be but foolishness and waste of time were it not for what I have in thee obtained to confirm the solemn contract. For were it not that thou art my God, my promises would be but idle words. I could fulfill nothing which my mouth has uttered and my pen has written. But since thou, Al-

> mighty, Omniscient, Omnipresent, and Eternal God, are mine, I have a thousandfold assurance that all shall be fulfilled through thy fullness.
>
> My ignorance is fully supplied by thy own infinite wisdom. My utter weakness and inability to preserve myself from sin are abundantly supplied by thy omnipotence, to thy everlasting praise.
>
> Glory to thy holy name! Though I have solemnly pledged all things to thee, yet, as thou art my "all and in all," I have nothing to fear. Now, O Father! my God and Savior, I humbly pray thee so to keep me that all my powers of soul, body, and spirit, my time, talents, will, influence, words, and works shall continually, exclusively and eternally glorify thy holy name through Jesus Christ, my Lord and Savior. Amen and amen.
>
> In covenant with the God of all grace and mercy, who has become my salvation, my all, and whose I am forever, to the praise of his glory. Amen.
>
> Entered into by the direction of the Holy Spirit and signed this thirteenth day of December, in the year of our Lord eighteen hundred and seventy-seven. Daniel Sidney Warner.[7]

The idea of a written form of consecration did not originate with D. S. Warner. George Whitefield, the famous colleague of John Wesley, said:

7. A. L. Byers, *Birth of a Reformation,* pp. 145-147.

> I can call heaven and earth to witness that when the bishop laid his hands upon me, I gave myself up to be a martyr for Him who hung upon the cross for me. I have thrown myself blindfolded and without reserve into his Almighty hands.

Dr. Philip Doddridge (died 1751), famous English Independent Divine, author of many books, among them *The Rise and Progress of Religion in the Soul,* wrote out the following form of consecration:

> This day do I, with the utmost solemnity, surrender myself to thee. I renounce all former lords that have had dominion over me; and I consecrate to thee all that I am, and all that I have; the faculties of my mind, the members of my body, my worldly possessions, my time and my influence over others; to be all used entirely for thy glory, and resolutely employed in obedience to thy commands, as long as thou continuest me in life; with an ardent desire and humble resolution to be thine through the endless ages of eternity; ever holding myself in an attentive posture to observe the first intimations of thy will, and ready to spring forward with zeal and joy to the immediate execution of it.
>
> To thy direction also I resign myself, and all I am and have, to be disposed of by thee in such a manner as thou shalt in thine infinite wisdom judge most subservient to the purposes of thy glory. To thee I leave

> the management of all events, and say without reserve, NOT my will but thine be done.[8]

The famous Baptist evangelist, Rev. A. B. Earle, prepared a blank book, which he called his consecration book, and on bended knee slowly and solemnly wrote in it the following dedication:

> ANDOVER,
> February 10, 1859
>
> This day I make a new consecration of my all to Christ. Jesus, I now and forever give myself to thee; my soul to be washed in thy blood and saved in heaven at last; my whole body to be used for thy glory; my mouth to speak for thee at all times; my eyes to weep over lost sinners, or to be used for any purpose for thy glory; my feet to carry me where thou shalt wish me to go; my heart to be burdened for souls or used for thee anywhere; my intellect to be employed at all times for thy cause and glory; I give to thee my wife, my children, my property, all I have, and all that ever shall be mine. I will obey thee in every known duty.
>
> I then asked for grace to enable me to carry out that vow, and that I might take nothing from the altar.[9]

A helpful form of thoughtful consecration and pledge of faith was drawn by Rev. Isaiah Reid as follows:

---

8. Philip Doddridge, *The Rise and Progress of Religion in the Soul,* chap. 17.
9. A. B. Earle, *Rest of Faith,* pp. 67-68.

Form for Consecration for Holiness

Text: Rom. 12:1-2. O Lord, in view of this thing thou hast besought me to do, I hereby now do really consecrate myself unreservedly to thee for all time and eternity. My time, my talents, my hands, feet, lips, will, my all. My property, my reputation, my entire being, a living sacrifice to be and to do all thy righteous will pertaining to me....Especially at this time do I, thy regenerate child, put my case into thy hands for the cleansing of my nature from the inherited taint of the carnal nature. I seek the sanctification of my soul.

Then he added the following:

Pledge of Faith

Now, as I have given myself away, I will, from this time forth, regard myself as thine. I believe thou dost accept the offering that I bring. I put all on the altar. I believe the altar sanctifieth the gift. I believe the blood is applied now as I comply with the terms of thy salvation. I believe that thou dost now cleanse me from all sin.

Vow

By thy grace, from this time forth, I promise to follow thee, walking in the fellowship of the Spirit, perfecting holiness in the fear of the Lord.

Name
Date

These forms of consecration seek to make the vows more vivid by particularizing all of the items of a man's possessions, and doubtless this may be helpful as a plow going to the roots of personality, but it is well to remember that in reality the thing that is consecrated, is one's self. His soul, his personality and, as Prof. Dougan Clark has said, "The essence of consecration is in the sentence, 'yield yourselves unto God.' If you yield yourself, you yield everything else. All the details are included in the one surrender of yourself. Yield yourself unto God. Consecration is not to God's service, not to his work, not to a life of obedience and sacrifice, not to the church, not to the Christian Endeavor, not to the missionary cause, nor even to the cause of God. It is to God himself. Yield yourself to God and your work, your service, your obedience, your sacrifice, your right place and your allotted duty will all follow in good time. Consecration is the willingness and the resolution, the purpose to be and to do and to suffer all God's will. Consecration being a definite transaction and made once for all does not need to be repeated unless we have failed to keep it. We consecrate just as we are married. The vow is upon us and in the force of that vow we walk all of our days."[10]

CONSECRATION AS INVESTMENT

No doubt the Wesleyan doctrine of entire sanctification has suffered much persecution because it is such a high and pre-

10. A. M. Hills, *Holiness and Power*, p. 252.

cious spiritual truth that the devil would bankrupt hell in order to destroy it. Nevertheless, one cannot help feeling a suspicion that the preachers of the doctrine and many who claim the experience have, by wrong presentation and imperfect living, done an injury to the doctrine that could not have been accomplished by Satan in direct attack. One of these mistakes has been that so many preachers and workers have stressed the negative side of sanctification and of consecration. We have preached about *giving up* and of *dying*, until many careless listeners have thought that perhaps that is about all there is to it—that sanctification is a doctrine of negation, a kind of asceticism, a kind of denial of life. Nearly all thoughtful Christians have seen the danger of overemphasizing any part of the Christian religion as self-sacrifice, whereas its true meaning is privilege. On two occasions I have visited Palestine and walked through old Jerusalem near the place where the Son of God bore the heavy cross and the burden of men's sorrows and sin; and when I stood in that sacred spot, it seemed to me altogether unsuitable any more to talk about "my sacrifice" in view of his sacrifice for me upon the cross. It seems to me that every Christian ought to begin to pray God to help us see more clearly and preach more powerfully the sacrifice of Christ and say less about our own small sacrifices.

In saying this not one word is retracted about giving up, dying out, and consecrating as part of the act of faith which accepts the baptism of the Holy Ghost and of power. But I see this consecration more and more, not in the light of loss, but of investment for unmeasured gain. Every young man who is to attain any kind of prominence or success in the world will find it necessary to invest his life in one certain kind of effort. Sometimes this decision is reached merely through what the world calls the force of circumstance, or what Christians call Providential direction—a certain kind of work opens up to a man and he goes along with it without much consideration. Those who attain great distinction usually make their choice in a crisis of stern, earnest, sober thought. Young men who wish to be doctors must consecrate themselves to long years of strenuous toil, and the same may be said for those preparing to be engineers, lawyers, or to follow other professions.

A boy's decision to study science when he would like to be playing ball or having fun with the other boys might be called a kind of consecration; but those who make this kind of consecration never seem to ask anybody's pity. They feel that they are investors and that the returns will be satisfactory. All Christians who seek a deeper work of grace should take the same view of consecration. Not sacrifice, but privilege is the key word of this experience.

Many years ago there was a famous negro woman evangelist, Amanda Smith, who traveled nearly all over the world and enjoyed a fame and success very few scholarly ministers could match. She reached this glorious privilege by the road of consecration, and this is the way she told it: "You must make your consecration complete and you must make it eternal. No experimenting by temporary consecration will answer. It must be complete and eternal. I gave everything to God. All that I had was my black self and my washtub and my washboard, but I gave all, and the Spirit came and sanctified my soul."

Consecration strikes the rock from which the waters of success flow. It is not loss, but wise investment.

THE FAITH THAT ACCEPTS HOLINESS

Entire sanctification is not so utterly different from justification by faith that its reception by faith should require a different set of principles and doctrinal proof. Once we have established the fact that entire sanctification is a definite crisis experience in the work of human redemption we should require texts to prove that faith is not necessary rather than to prove it necessary. It is an axiom of evangelical theology that all the redemptive work of Christ is a gift, and as such is not attainable as a reward of merit or pay for the vast labor of painful work, but is a gracious favor given into the receptive hands of active and childlike faith. This ought to be apparent to every convinced believer in New Testament Christianity. No justification without faith, no sanctification without faith, no justification by works, no sanctification by works. "By grace are ye saved through faith," and we cannot be saved otherwise. In the New Testament the principle is made for every simple, earnest, Christian heart that faith is the condition of all the blessings of the atonement. "As Moses lifted up the serpent in the wilderness, even so must the Son of man be lifted up; that whosoever believeth in him should not perish, but have eternal life" (John 3:14-15). "He that heareth my word, and believeth on him that sent me, hath everlasting life" (John 5:24). In these texts faith is the condition of accepting the benefits of the atoning work of Christ.

The only work which God requires for the reception of his redemption blessing is faith. "This is the work of God, that ye believe on him whom he hath sent" (John 6:29). "Thy faith hath made thee whole" (Matt. 9:22). "According to your faith be it unto you" (vs. 29). Paul was an entirely sanctified man, and he testified: "I am crucified with Christ: nevertheless I live; yet not I, but Christ liveth in me: and the life which I now live in the flesh I live by the faith of the Son of God" (Gal. 2:20).

"And put no difference between us and them, purifying their hearts by faith" (Acts 15:9). Here the purifying baptism of the Holy Spirit is credited to the receptive act of faith. "That they may receive forgiveness of sins, and inheritance among them which are sanctified by faith that is in me" (Acts 26:18). "Every man that hath this hope in him purifieth himself, even as he is pure" (I John 3:3). The man with hope in him is a Christian man, and this Christian man purifies himself by the faith which accepts entire sanctification. "God hath from the beginning chosen you to salvation through sanctification of the Spirit and belief of the truth" (II Thess. 2:13).

For two hundred years saints have sung with captivating melody, preached with prophetic power, and witnessed with seraphic life to the glory, the joy, and the power of this uttermost salvation. The gospel of perfect love and full salvation cannot be destroyed any more than men can destroy geometry, trigonometry, and calculus. Men may forget these sciences until they have sunk into barbarism, but if ever they enjoy noble buildings, complicated machinery, and modern civilization they must revive these sciences; and if the church will ever know, or wish to know, the glory and the power and the victory of New Testament Christianity it must revive the gospel of full salvation.

APPENDIX

THE THIRTY TEXTS OF WESLEY

Many years ago it was discovered that John Wesley based his doctrine on entire sanctification almost entirely upon thirty texts in the Bible. Of course, it is foolish to suggest that thirty texts are not enough to establish a doctrine; for even one text would be sufficient if all obscurity were removed. Dr. W. E. Sangster has treated these texts separately in his book *The Path to Perfection.* The references are given here in order that students may have a compact array of scriptural evidence on the subject. It is not meant, however, to indicate my personal agreement with Wesley regarding the meaning of each text, nor would this listing rule out other texts. This list is merely given for what it is worth:

> Ezekiel 36:25-26, 29; Matthew 5:8, 48; 6:10; John 3:36; 5:24; 6:47; 8:34ff; 27:20-23; Romans 2:29; 12:1; 13:12; I Corinthians 4:3ff; 11:31ff; II Corinthians 3:17ff; 7:1; Galatians 2:20; Ephesians 3:14-19; Philippians 3:15; I Thessalonians 2:10; 5:23; Titus 2:11-14; Hebrews 6:1; 7:25; 10:14; James 1:4; I John 1:5, 7; 2:6; 3:3, 8-10; 5:8-9, 13.

ARE WE SAVED TO THE UTTERMOST?

Possibly millions of sermons have been preached on this famous text: "Wherefore he is able also to save them to the uttermost that come unto God by him, seeing he ever liveth to make intercession for them" (Heb. 7:25). But when the preacher of today takes up his modern English translation and reads this text he finds himself at a loss, for in some modern speech versions it is translated to mean that Christ saves forever those who come to him. Thus the word which in the Authorized Version is rendered "uttermost" is made to express duration, and not completeness.

What are the facts? The Greek word here translated "uttermost" is *panteles,* and it occurs only twice in the New Testament—in the passage under consideration and in Luke 13:11. In the latter passage it means "completely." "Behold there was a woman who had a spirit of infirmity eighteen years, and was bowed together, and utterly unable to lift up herself." In their vocabulary of the Greek New Testament Moulton and Milligan cite numerous instances from the papyri in which this word is used to indicate now completeness and now duration. So this is again another one of those cases where the translator was thrown back upon his own judgment. He was not bound by the sources to take either one of these meanings, but had a choice.

It is easy to see why some of the modern translators were led to the idea of duration. In Hebrews 7, Christ is contrasted with the priests of the old law. They were priests who had infirmity; Christ was a perfected priest. They were "not suffered to continue by reason of death," but he had an unchangeable priesthood. To indicate this temporal contrast the translators interpreted the word *panteles* to mean "forever." But they might just as well have translated it "completely" or "utterly," in conformity with abundance of authority and a perfectly reasonable reading of the context of the passage. In that context we note other contrasts besides that of time. Christ is not only greater than the priests of the Jewish law because he lives forever, but he is also greater because he is not subject to their weakness and incompleteness. Note the weakness of the Jewish priesthood standing in contrast with Christ's perfection. They are made after the law of carnal commandments (vs. 16). Their system was weak and unprofitable (vs. 18). It made nothing perfect (vs. 19). Their priests were made without an oath (vs. 21). There were many of them, but only one Christ (vs. 23). They had to offer for their own sins (vs. 27), and they had infirmities (vs. 28). By implication they were unholy, defiled, and by nature sinners (vs. 26). These considerations show us how unnecessary it is to construe the "utterly" of verse 25 as pertaining to the *time* of Christ's priesthood, when it might as well be construed as pertaining to its quality, its perfectness.

In at least three modern English Testaments this word is translated "utterly," that is, as indicating that Christ's salvation is complete and perfect. Following are the names of men who have translated it thus: Dr. Ferrar Fenton, Dr. R. F. Weymouth, and a group of modern scholars who translated the *Twentieth Century New Testament.* And with them agrees the famous English commentator and scholar, Dean Henry Alford. On this passage he writes: "He is able to save (in its usual solemn New Testament sense, to rescue from sin and condemnation) *to the uttermost.* Some take this of *time:* 'He is ever able to save,' or, 'He is able to save forever.' But this is not the usage of the word. Bleek has shown by very many instances that *completeness,* not *duration,* is its idea."[1]

The many other passages of the New Testament glorifying Christ as a perfect Savior and exalting the great salvation give us ample assurance that we are safe in interpreting this term as describing a complete and perfect salvation, not only endless in duration, but perfect in its nature.

1. Henry Alford, *The New Testament for English Readers,* Vol. II, p. 672.

PAUL'S EXHORTATION TO THE EPHESIANS

"And it came to pass, that, while Apollos was at Corinth, Paul having passed through the upper coasts came to Ephesus: and finding certain disciples, he said unto them, Have ye received the Holy Ghost since ye believed? And they said unto him, We have not so much as heard whether there be any Holy Ghost....When they heard this, they were baptized in the name of the Lord Jesus, and when Paul had laid his hands upon them, the Holy Ghost came on them" (Acts 19:2, 5-6).

Wesleyan preachers have long used Paul's question: "Have ye received the Holy Ghost since ye believed?" as evidence that the Holy Spirit is received after the experience of believing for regeneration. When, therefore, many modern translations revised this to read, "Did ye receive the Holy Spirit when ye believed?" this change was used as an argument against the doctrine of sanctification as a second work of grace.

Owing to its technical nature this matter has not been discussed in the text of this book. However, there can be no objection to such a discussion in an appendix, where only those interested need read it. I think, too, that it is a popular question—not, indeed, with the godless and worldly who despise all such discussions as trivial, but with those spiritual people who are in deep earnest about holiness, even if they cannot read Greek. And such people are entitled to know that there are strong reasons for accepting the older translation of the Authorized Version, which reads "since."

In the first place, the new translation is not due to critical changes in the text. Before me there lies the newly revised sixteenth edition (1936) of Nestle's text based upon Westcott and Hort, Tischendorf, B. Weiss, Von Soden, and many newly discovered manuscripts. At this point the wording is the same as the one used by the translators of the Authorized Version. As free from grammatical technicalities as possible, the discussion follows.

In the Greek the critical passage reads as literally translated into English, "Spirit Holy received ye having believed?" "Having believed" is here the aorist participle. The question is, to make this good English should we say "since ye believed" or "when ye believed"? I maintain that the sense is "having believed"; or, "After ye believed did ye receive the Holy Ghost?" The believing was first. The proof of this for the English reader is found in the fact that the same construction is used in the context in the Greek. "Paul having passed through the upper coasts came to Ephesus," Here the "having passed" is likewise the aorist participle. Would you say that Paul came to Ephesus at the very same instant when he was passing through the upper coasts, or after he passed through the upper coasts? "After," of course, is the meaning of the passage.

Note again: "And having found certain disciples, he said to them." Here the "having found" is likewise the aorist participle. If we should translate that Paul said something to the disciples *when* he found them, we should mean actually *after* he found them; for he had to find them before he could say anything to them. The point insisted on here is that the real meaning is the same in all these cases. Paul came to Ephesus *after* he passed through the upper coasts. He spoke to the disciples *after* he found them, and these disciples were asked whether they had received the Holy Ghost *after* they had believed.

To change the form of the question: Does the main verb ("did ye receive?") refer to a time after that of the participle ("having believed") or co-incident with it? A. T. Robertson, who was one of the foremost New Testament Greek scholars of our time, taught New Testament Greek for many years and was familiar with the Papyri Manuscripts which forced a rewriting of Greek grammar and a recasting of the exegesis of the Greek New Testament. His famous and massive grammar of the Greek New Testament was written in the light of the papyri discoveries and the *Koine.*

It is true that Dr. Robertson thought the time of the main verb here ("did you receive?") and of the participle ("having believed") to be coincident, but in his crystal honesty he gives us good reason to think otherwise. He says, "The antecedent use furnishes the largest number of instances." Here he means that in the majority of cases in the New Testament the participle ("having believed") refers to a time antecedent to the main verb ("did ye receive?") And he quotes from J. H. Moulton: "The participle naturally came to involve past time relative to that of the main verb."[2] Again quoting from Dr. Robertson: "*Antecedent action.* This is the usual idiom with the circumstantial participle. This is indeed the most common use of the aorist participle." As examples he cites: Matt. 4:2; 27:3, 5; Mark 1:31; Col. 1:3-4; Acts 17:31; Heb. 1. The reader of Greek can easily find the participles and verbs here. For the English reader, here is a hint as to how to find them.

2. A. T. Robertson, *A Grammar of the Greek New Testament,* p. 1112.

Matthew 4:4 in the Greek reads "and having fasted ...afterward he hungered."

Examples of simultaneous action are given by Dr. Robertson as follows: Luke 5:4; Matt. 2:8; 22:1; 27:4; Acts 15:8. Scrutiny of these texts proves that the time of the main verb and participle is identical. But some texts in the New Testament seem doubtful. How shall one decide? Dr. Robertson says very candidly: "In many examples only exegesis can determine whether antecedent or coincident action is intended as in Hebrews 9:12."[3]

We praise the candor of a great Christian scholar who admits that the translator's beliefs must influence his translation at times. He also suggests that the decision involves a question of judgment, and not some intricacy of the Greek language. James Moffatt, another great Christian scholar, is equally candid and fair. He says in the introduction to his translation of the Bible: "A real translation is in the main an interpretation."[4]

And people who can read Greek prize Moffatt for his brilliant interpretations of familiar texts. Often these interpretations introduce ideas never heard of before in that connection. In the "when" translation, however, we have an interpretation fully in harmony with the modern Protestant church tradition that holds that the Holy Spirit baptism is received at the instant of regeneration. Nevertheless, this interpretation is at variance with the ancient Catholic tradition, which, as could be shown by dozens of quotations, has always

3. Ibid., pp. 860-1.

4. Page vii.

held that the gift of the Holy Spirit is received after regeneration, that is, after baptism where baptism is believed to effect, or at least coincide with, regeneration. Review the history of confirmation for evidence.

The point is conceded by *The Expositor's Greek Testament,* which while it translates "when" instead of "since" does admit that as disciples these men were real Christians before receiving the Holy Ghost. "The question was whether they had received the Holy Ghost at their Baptism."[5] This is all I contend for, because the other converts received the Holy Ghost after their conversion, whether we believe with evangelical Protestants that people are first converted and then baptized or with the Catholics that baptism effects regeneration.

Even if "when" is used in this passage it still disproves the point it is used to support. It stands on the face of the narrative here that the disciples at Ephesus actually did not receive the Holy Ghost at the identical time of their believing, or conversion; for by his language Paul admits that they are believers and at the same time he prayed for them that they might receive the Holy Ghost—after he had admitted that they were believers.

For these reasons we may feel indifferent about the "when" translation; for it will bear a loose construction, allowing for a passage of time between the action of the main verb and the participle. As one might say, "When I went to California I bought an orange grove." Here the time is indefinite. Evidently very few people would buy an orange grove the first

5. Vol. 11, p. 403.

day they arrived; however, such an expression is quite as common as "After I went to California I bought an orange grove."

That this is the meaning of the passage in Acts 19:2 is one of the most certain points in scriptural interpretation; if doubt arises as to the exact order of the time of the reception of the Holy Ghost by the disciples at Ephesus that question is to be settled by appeal to similar instances in the Book of Acts itself, and here the evidence is overwhelmingly convincing to any unbiased reader who will accept the authority of the book. "And they were all filled with the Holy Ghost" (Acts 2:4). In chapter VII evidence amounting to proof has been given that these people were and had been definite believers long before this event. "When they believed Philip preaching the things concerning the kingdom of God, and the name of Jesus Christ, they were baptized, both men and women....Now when the apostles which were at Jerusalem heard that Samaria had received the word of God, they sent unto them Peter and John: who, when they were come down, prayed for them, that they might receive the Holy Ghost" (8:12-15). Here it is plainly stated that these people became believers and were baptized under the ministry of one evangelist and later received the baptism of the Holy Ghost under the ministry of two other evangelists. This was certainly *after* they believed or only in a very loose sense of the word when they believed. When Peter was preaching in Cornelius' house, while he "yet spake these words, the Holy Ghost fell on all them which heard the word" (Acts 10:44). This gift of the Holy Ghost was given to people who already believed and knew the word of God concerning salvation in Christ (10:36-37).

By reference to these three definite instances in which people received the Holy Ghost after they believed, and by the clear evidence that the disciples at Ephesus actually did not receive the Holy Ghost at the identical time when they believed, we have reached the conclusion that the translation "Did ye receive the Holy Ghost when ye believed" is to be understood as "Did ye receive the Holy Ghost at that season of your life when you began your career of discipleship, that is, within a short time after your baptism?" That is the time when the others received the Holy Ghost. To these same people the Apostle Paul later wrote: "In whom also after that ye believed, ye were sealed with that Holy Spirit of promise" (Eph. 1:13).

THE TENSE READINGS OF THE GREEK NEW TESTAMENT[6]

By Dr. Daniel Steele, for many years professor of New Testament Greek in Boston University School of Theology.

In this age of astonishing scientific progress, when the microscope applied to living tissues reveals whole continents of evidences of design in bioplastic life, and marvelously strengthens theism in its debate with atheism, we have applied the same instrument to the Greek Testament, in the aid of exegesis, in the interest of disputed truths, and for the refutation of certain doctrinal errors. Our microscope will be directed to a long-neglected field of research, the Greek tenses, not for the purpose of discovering new truths, but for the confirmation and clear elucidation of verities as old as revelation.... That the English scholar may understand our argument and our illustrations we will give the following definitions: The present tense denotes what is now going on, and indicates a continuous, repeated, or habitual action, as *I am writing.* The imperfect denotes the same continuity or repetition in the past, as, *I was writing.*

"The aorist indicative," says Goodwin, "expresses the simple *momentary* occurrence of an action in past time, as *I wrote.*" The perfect denotes an action as already finished at the present time, as, *I have written;* my writing is just now finished. It also expresses the continuance of the result down to the present time; as the formula "It is written" is literally *it has been written,* and implies that it now stands on record; the

6. Daniel Steele, *Mile-Stone Papers,* pp. 53-90. (Italics are the author's.)

door *has been shut,* that is, it so remains till now. The pluperfect denotes an act which took place before another past act.

The chief peculiarity lies in the aorist. We have in the English no tense like it. Except in the indicative, it is timeless, and in all the moods indicates what Krueger styles "singleness of act." This idea our translators could not express without a circumlocution in words having no representatives in the Greek. "The poverty of our language," says Alford, "in the finer distinctions of the tenses, often obliges us to render inaccurately and fall short of the wonderful language with which we have to deal." His annotations abound in attempts to bring out the full significance of the tenses. For instance, in II Corinthians 12:7, *"to buffet"* (pres.) *me,* "is best thus expressed in the *present.* The aorist would denote but *one* such *act* of insult." This has been noted by both Chysostom and Theophylact....

Says Buttmann: "The established distinction between the aorist, as a purely narrative tense (expressing something momentary), and the imperfect as a descriptive tense (expressing something contemporaneous or continuous), holds in all its force in the New Testament." Says Winer: "Nowhere in the New Testament does the aorist express what is wont to be." In applying these principles we make several important discoveries. We cite only a few specimens:

1. All exhortations to prayer and to spiritual endeavor in the resistance of temptation are usually expressed in the present tense, which strongly indicates persistence.

Matt. 7:7: "Keep asking [pres.], and it shall be given you; seek [pres.] again and again, and ye shall find; knock persistently, and it shall be opened unto you."

Mark 11:24 (Alford's version): "Therefore I say unto you, All things that ye perseveringly pray [pres.], and ask for [pres.], keep believing [pres.] that ye received [aor., Alford], and ye shall have them."

Luke 11:10: "For every one that asketh [pres.] perseveringly, receiveth; and he that seeketh [pres.] untiringly, findeth; and to him that persistently knocketh [pres.], it shall be opened." Verse 13: "How much more shall your heavenly Father give the Holy Spirit to them that importunately ask [pres.] him." The idea implied is clearly expressed in Luke 18:1.

John 16:24: "Ask [pres.] repeatedly, and ye shall receive, that your joy may be permanently filled" [perfect].

Luke 13:24: "Persistently agonize to enter in [aor.], once for all, at the strait gate."

Luke 18:13: "But he kept smiting [imperfect] and saying, God be merciful [aor.] to me, the sinner." The conditions of pardon are persistently complied with.

James 1:5-6: "If any of you lack wisdom, let him frequently ask [pres.] of God...But let him ask [pres.] repeatedly in faith, etc. Heb. 11:6: "For he that persistently comes [pres.] to God must believe [aor., definitely grasp two facts] (1) that God exists, and (2) that he is becoming a rewarder to those who diligently and repeatedly seek him."

To this use of the present tense a remarkable exception occurs in Christ's last address before his crucifixion, John 14:16. Here he for the first time directs us to pray in his name, and, as if to denote the influence of that all-prevailing name when presented to the Father in faith, the aorist tense is used when prayer is commanded, as if to teach that one presentation of the name of the adorable Son of God must be successful. See John 14:13-14, and 16:23-24. In the twenty-third verse the aorist occurs, but in verse 24 the present tense (be asking) is used, probably in view of the foreseen fact that there would be multitudes of half-believers, who must be encouraged to pray till they fully believe in the name of Jesus Christ.

2. The next fact which impresses us in our investigation is *the absence of the aorist and the presence of the present tense whenever the conditions of final salvation are stated.* Our inference is that the conditions of ultimate salvation are continuous, extending through probation, and not completed in any one act. The great requirement is faith in Jesus Christ. A careful study of the Greek will convince the student that it is a great mistake to teach that a single act of faith furnishes a person with a paid-up, nonforfeitable policy, assuring the holder that he will inherit eternal life, or that a single energy of faith secures a through ticket for heaven, as is taught by the Plymouth Brethren and by some popular lay evangelists. The Greek tenses show that faith is a state, a habit of mind, into which the believer enters at justification. The widespread mistake on this point is thus illustrated by Dr. John Hall, of New York;

> Have you ever seen a young girl learn to fire a pistol? I will not say, imagine a boy, for he would naturally be brave about it. I have seen young ladies acquiring this accomplishment, and it is a very curious thing. It may illustrate to you the false notion that many persons have about faith. The pistol is loaded and handed to

> the young lady. She takes hold of it very 'gingerly,' as if afraid it may shoot from the handle. Now, she means to go through with it; there is the mark: so she takes the pistol in her hand, and holds it out a long way, and appears to take aim with the greatest exactness, but does not shoot. She is a little afraid, trembles, and holds back. At last she screws up her courage to the sticking point, and, as you suppose, taking the most exact aim, shuts her eyes firmly, and fires. The thing is done, and done with. Well, now, many intelligent persons are led to believe that faith is something like that—something you end in an instant. You screw up your courage for it, then shut your eyes, and just believe once for all; then the thing is done, and you are saved. Now, that is a mistaken idea about faith itself. That real faith which is honest goes on from time to eternity.

Since we are writing for the English readers, we will refrain from quoting the Greek verbs, which would make our pages repulsive to the very class which we wish to benefit. Scholars will appreciate our argument if they accompany it with their Greek Testaments.

John 1:12: "But as many as received [aor.] him [by a momentary and definite act], to them gave he power to become the sons of God, even to them that are believing [pres.] perseveringly on his name." Here the aorist participle would have been used instead of the present, if a single act of faith secured ultimate salvation.

John 3:15: "That whosoever is continuously believing in him should not perish [aor., once for all], but be having everlasting life." Here, again, the present and not the aorist participle of the verb to *believe* is used, as it is again in verses 16 and 36.

John 5:24: "Verily, verily I say unto you, he that is always hearing my word, and constantly believing on him that sent me, hath eternal life, and is not coming into condemnation, but has passed over [perfect] from death unto life, and so continues." Says Alford: "So in I John 5:12-13, the believing and the having eternal life are *commensurate;* where the faith is, the possession of eternal life is, and when the one remits, the other is forfeited. But here the faith is set before us as an *enduring* faith, and its effects described *in their completion.* (See Eph. 1:19-20.)" Thus this great English scholar rescues this chief proof text of the Plymouth Brethren and the Moody school of evangelists from its perverted use, to teach an eternal incorporation into Christ by a single act of faith, and he demonstrates the commonsense doctrine that the perseverance of the saints is grounded on persistent trust in Jesus Christ. A wise generalship does not destroy a captured fortress, but garrisons it.

John 5:44: "How are ye able to put forth a momentary act of faith [aor.] who habitually receive [pres.] honor one of another, and are not constantly seeking the honor which is from God only?" This interrogatory implies the impossibility of a single genuine act of faith springing up in a heart persistently courting human applause.

John 5:47: "But if ye are not habitually believing his writings, how will ye believe my words?"

John 6:29: The received text reads thus: "This is the work of God, that ye believe [aor., once for all] on him whom he sent." When we first noticed this aorist tense, implying that the whole work required by God is summed up in an isolated act, we felt that there must be an error in this tense. By referring to Alford, Tregelles, and Tischendorf, we find that the aorist is rejected, and the present tense is restored, so that it reads: "This is the work of God, that ye perseveringly believe," etc.

John 6:35: "He that is perpetually coming [pres.] to me shall not, by any means [double negative], once hunger [aor.], and he that is constantly believing in ME [emphatic] shall never, by any means [double negative], feel one pang of thirst" [aor.].

John 6:54: "Whose eateth [pres., keeps eating] my flesh, and drinketh [keeps drinking] my blood, hath eternal life."

John 11:25-26: "He that believeth persistently [pres.] shall not, by any means [double negative], die [aor.] forever."

John 20:31: "That ye might believe [aor.; but Tischendorf has the present, continue to believe] that Jesus is the Christ, the Son of God, and that, believing constantly [pres.], ye might have life through his name."

Acts 26:30-31: "Sirs, what must I do to be instantaneously saved [aor.]? Believe instantaneously [aor.] on the Lord Jesus." This is no exception to the general use of the tenses. The jailer wished immediate deliverance from his guilt, and was directed to a definite and sharply defined act of reliance on Christ. But in Romans 1:16 where future and eternal salvation is spoken of, it is promised to every one that perseveringly believes [pres.]. So also in Romans 3:22; 4:24; 9:33; 10:11; I Cor. 1:21; Eph. 1:19; I Thess. 2:10, 13; 4:14.

In II Thessalonians 1:10 we find, not in the received text, but in the best manuscripts, an exceptional instance of the use of the aorist in expressing the conditions of final salvation: "to be admired in all them that believe" [aor.]. Alford says it is used because the writer is "looking back from that day on the past," probation being viewed as a point.

A similar explanation he gives to the aorist in Hebrews 4:3, saying, that the standpoint is the day of entering into the rest. We prefer to teach that the aorist is preferred to the present in this passage because the general state of trust is not under discussion as the condition of entering eternal rest in heaven, but the grasping of the definite fact of Christ's ability to be the believer's Joshua, and to bring him into soul-rest in the present life. Hence the exhortation, verse 11, "Let us labor [Greek, *hasten*] to enter [aor.] into that rest." Other instances of the aorist, used when some distinct saying is to be believed, are found in John 4:21; and in Matthew 8:13.

Rev. 22:14: "Blessed are they that are constantly doing his commandments, that they may have right to the tree of life, and may enter through the gates into the city." The best manuscripts read, "Blessed are they that are always washing their garments," etc. In both instances the present tense is used. This is the last time the conditions of final salvation are expressed in the Bible....

Hence we conclude, from a thorough examination of the above texts, that the spirit of inspiration has uniformly chosen the present tense in order to teach that final salvation depends on persevering faith.

3. But when we come to consider *work of purification* in the believer's soul, by the power of the Holy Spirit, both in the new birth and in entire sanctification, we find that *the aorist is almost uniformly used.* This tense, according to the best New Testament grammarians, never indicates a continuous, habitual, or repeated act, but one which is momentary, and done once for all. We adduce a few illustrative passages:

Matt. 8:2-3: "And behold, there came a leper, and he kept worshiping [imperfect] him, saying, Lord, if thou wilt thou canst cleanse [aor.] me once for all. And Jesus, stretching out [aor.] his hand, touched [aor.] him, saying, I will, be thou instantaneously cleansed" [aor.]. The leper prayed to be cleansed, not gradually, but instantly, and it was done at a stroke, according to his faith.

Matthew 14:36 illustrates the difference between the imperfect and the aorist: "And they kept beseeching [imp.] that they might touch just once [aor.] only the hem of his garment; and as many as only once touched [aor.] were instantaneously healed" [aor.].

Matt. 23:25-26: "Woe unto you scribes and Pharisees, hypocrites; for ye are constantly cleansing [pres.] the outside of the cup and the platter, but within are full of extortion and injustice. Thou blind Pharisee, first cleanse [aor.] at a stroke the inside of the cup and of the platter, that the outside may instantly become [aor.] clean also." If Christ had commanded a gradual inward cleansing he would have used the present tense, "be cleansing by degrees."

Luke 17:14: "And it came to pass that while they were going [pres.] they were instantaneously healed" [aor.].

John 17:17-19: "Sanctify [aor., imperative] them once for all through thy truth, that is, through faith in the distinctive office and work of the Comforter.... And for their sakes I am consecrating [pres.] myself, in order that they in reality may have been permanently sanctified." Christ's was not a real sanctification or cleansing, inasmuch as he was never polluted; but the disciples needed sanctification *in reality*, or "truly." This is the suggested meaning of the words "through the truth." See Bagster's marginal reading. Compare II Corinthians 7:14. Says Winer: "In the New Testament the obvious distinction between the imperative aorist—as *sanctify*, above—and the imperative present is uniformly maintained. The imperative aorist denotes an action that is either rapidly completed and transient, or viewed as occurring but once. The imperative present denotes an action already commenced and to be continued, or an action going on, or to be frequently repeated." Both the aorist and the present are sometimes used in the same sentence, as in John 2:16: "Take [aor.] these things hence instantly, and be not making [pres.] my Father's house a house of merchandise." I Cor. 15:34: "Awake [aor.], and be not sinning" [pres.], or "stop sinning." Acts 15:11: "But we habitually believe that through the grace of the Lord Jesus Christ we were saved [aor., by a momentary and completed act], even as they" [saved from guilt, not saved eternally]. Rom. 6:13: Here occurs a beautiful instance of this distinction, affording an undoubted proof text for instantaneous sanctification, which is not seen in the English version:

"Nor render repeatedly [present imperative] your members as instruments of unrighteousness to sin; but render [aor., by a final act of unreserved surrender, once for all] yourselves [not your members by a repeated and piecemeal consecration] to God [or for God's cause, says Tholuck], as alive from the dead." Says Alford: "The present imperative above denotes *habit;* the exhortation guards against the recurrence of a devotion of the members to sin; this aorist imperative, on the other hand, as in chap. 12:1, denotes an *act* of self-devotion to God *once for all,* not a mere recurrence of the habit." Tholuck's annotation brings out the completeness of this text as a proof of cleansing from original sin....

Rom. 12:1: "That ye present [aor.] your bodies" [as a single act, never needing to be repeated]. The body is specified, because, says Tholuck, it is the organ of practical activity, or, as Olshausen, De Wette, and Alford say, "as an indication that the sanctification of Christian life is to extend to that part of man's nature which is most completely under bondage to sin." If in Paul's conception believers were to be sinning and repenting all their days, as the best that grace could do for them, he would have used the present imperative, "Be presenting your bodies again and again." In Alford's note on I Peter 2:5, he says: "The aorist is here used, because no habitual offering, as in rite or festival, is meant, but the one, once for all, devotion of the body, as in Romans 12:1, to God as his." Both of these are proof texts of a sharply defined transition in Christian experience, called entire consecration, the human part of entire sanctification. That neither of these texts refers to justification is shown (1) by the fact that the persons addressed are already Christians; (2) by the requirement that the sacrifice be *holy* (Rom. 12:1), that is, accepted, as the lamb was examined by the priest, and pronounced fit for sacrifice, or acceptable to Jehovah; and I Peter 2:5 requires a holy or accepted priesthood, both of which requirements symbolize a state of justification before God.

Rom. 13:14: "Put ye on [aor., a single definite act] the Lord Jesus Christ, and make [pres.] not [that is, quit making] provision for the flesh," etc.

Acts 15:9: "Instantaneously purifying [aor.] their hearts by faith." This verse is a key to the instantaneous sanctifying work of the Holy Spirit wrought in the hearts of believers on the Day of Pentecost, since the words *even as he did unto us* refer to that occasion. See Acts 10:45-47.

I Cor. 5:7: "Purge out [aor.] the old leaven, that ye may be a new lump." This summary and instantaneous excision of the incestuous offender illustrates the force of the aorist in verbs signifying *to purify*.

I Cor. 6:11: "But ye washed yourselves [aor., middle] by submitting to outward baptism; ye were sanctified [aor.], ye were justified" [aor.]. Here the sanctification is a momentary and completed act, the same as the justification. By the figure called the inverted chiasmus the words "were justified" are placed last. The natural English order would be, "were justified in the name of the Lord Jesus, and were sanctified by the Spirit of our God." Rom. 6:6: "Knowing this, that our old man was crucified [aor.] once for all, that the body [being or totality] of sin might be destroyed [aor., at a stroke], that henceforth we should no longer be serving [pres.] sin. For he who once for all [aor.] died [unto sin] has been justified from sin."

The aorist here teaches the possibility of an instantaneous death-stroke to inbred sin, and that there is no need of a slow and painful process, lingering till physical death or purgatorial fires end the torment. Men are not crucified limb by limb, after one part is dead finding a hand or arm or finger alive, but the whole life is extinguished all at once. A class of interpreters, who are afraid of entire sanctification in this life, and are especially horrified at an instantaneous purification by the stroke of Omnipotence—Calvinists generally, and the Plymouth Brethren in particular—tone down the word "destroy" to "*render inoperative or powerless.*" The strength of this verb will be seen by studying the following texts, where it is rendered by "abolish," "consume," or "destroy." II Cor. 3:13; Eph. 2:15; II Tim. 1:10; I Cor. 6:13; 15:26; II Thess. 2:8; Heb. 2:14.

II Cor. 1:21-22: "Now, he who is continually establishing us with you, in Christ, and who once for all anointed [aor.] us, is God, who also sealed us [aor.] and gave [aor.] the earnest of the Spirit in our hearts." Here the stablishing is constant; the anointing, sealing, and endowment are momentary and completed acts. II Cor. 5:21: The received text reads, "That we might be made [pres., *being made*] the righteousness," etc.... This may refer to the redemption of the whole race, or to the transition of individuals into a state of holiness. Paul's use of the *we* favors the latter view. I Cor. 6:13: "Be ye also enlarged [aor.] by the sudden baptism of the Holy Spirit." II Cor. 7:1: "Let us cleanse [aor.] ourselves at a stroke from every filthiness of the flesh and spirit, perfecting [pres.] holiness in the fear of the Lord." If Paul had been exhorting to a gradual inward cleansing he would certainly have used the present tense. The chapter division is here very unfortunate, and very much obscures the writer's thought. Bengel puts this verse in the paragraph which closes the sixth chapter. The course of the argument is this: The promise of the Old Testament was that you should be sons and daughters of God. Having realized the fulfillment of this promise by adoption, let us who are sons cleanse ourselves, etc.

Cleansing is here viewed as a human work, inasmuch as our application of the purifying power is by faith, as we are to make unto ourselves new hearts by availing ourselves of the regenerating Spirit. Paul uses the adhortative form, "let us cleanse," instead of the exhortatory form, "cleanse ye," simply to soften the command by including himself. This beauty of Greek rhetoric could not be quoted to prove that the writer was polluted in the flesh and in the spirit, that is, was indulging in sensual and in spiritual sins. See James 3:5-6 and I Peter 4:3. The doctrine of this passage is that the faith that appropriates the Sanctifier is a momentary act, lifting the soul out of all outward or carnal, and inward or spiritual, sin. Had the process of sanctification been like washing a mud statue, a continuous and never completed work, as some teach, Paul would not have failed to express this idea by using the present tense: "Let us be continually cleansing," etc. While the Wesleyan doctrine of instantaneous sanctification is taught by the aorist tense in this verse, the seemingly paradoxical

Wesleyan doctrine of progressive sanctification is also taught by the present participle, "*perfecting*" holiness, etc.

This word in this passage is defined in Bagster's *Greek Testament Lexicon* thus, "to carry into practice, to realize." The perfect inward cleansing instantaneously wrought by the Holy Spirit through faith is to be constantly and progressively carried outward into all the acts of daily life, as the moral discrimination becomes more and more acute with the increase of knowledge.

Gal. 1:15-16: "But when it pleased God, who separated [aor.] me from my mother's womb, and called [aor.] me by his grace, to reveal [aor.] his Son in me," etc. The words rendered *separated* and *called* are aorist participles. Says Goodwin: "The aorist participle regularly refers to a momentary or single action, which is past with reference to the time of the leading verb." In this passage the leading verb is "*pleased.*" After his birth and calling, or conversion, there was an instantaneous revelation of the Son of God within, to the spiritual eye, as there had been an objective revelation of the form of the Son of man to Paul's physical eye on his way to Damascus. Both Ellicott and Alford insist that the sequence of tenses here teaches that this inward revelation of Christ was after his conversion. This is in harmony with Christ's promise that he would manifest himself to those who already love him and evince their love by their obedience (John 14:21; 16:14). This may well be styled Paul's second blessing.

Various metaphors and phrases are employed to denote entire sanctification, as will be seen in the following texts: Eph. 4:22: "That ye put off [aor.] the old man" [the unsanctified nature]. Here the aorist is used, because the act of putting off is one and decisive, "referring," says Alford, "to a direct, definite, and reflexive act." Verse 24: "And that ye put on [aor.] that new man, which after God is created [aor., was instantaneously created] in righteousness," etc. "Beware," says Alford, "of rendering, with Eadie and Peile, *'that ye have put off,'* which is inconsistent with the context (vs. 25), and not justified by the word 'you' being expressed." This epistle is addressed to the saints and the faithful in Christ Jesus (chap. 1:1). Such undoubted Christians are exhorted by one decisive act to lay off the old man, implying that he was not yet fully laid aside, and to put on the new man, as if Christ were not fully investing and pervading the nature. Why these aorists, if only a gradual growth out of sin into holiness is contemplated?

Gal. 2:19-20: "For I through the law died [aor., quite suddenly] to the law, that I might live unto God. I have been crucified [perfect] with Christ [and stay dead till now], and it is no longer I that live, but Christ that liveth in me." Says Alford: "The punctuation in the English version is altogether wrong." Here is a perfect answer, in Paul's testimony, to the advocates of a lingering death of the old man, continuing up to the separation of soul and body. There was a time when Paul died to sin by a crucifixion—a short and sharp kind of death—and the old man lived no more.

Some people are forever on the cross, always dying but never dead, because they do not grasp the sin-slaying power.

Gal. 5:24: "And they that are Christ's crucified [aor.] the flesh, together with the passions and lusts." From this it would appear that all believers are entirely sanctified as soon as they are regenerated. But Olshausen's explanation is very satisfactory. "It is remarkable here that the act of crucifying is designated as past, while it is, certainly, involved in the exhortations of Paul that it is to be continued. This is explained by the fact that Paul here presents the idea of a true Christian quite objectively, and, therefore, *in its completeness;* as such, the believer has *entirely crucified* the flesh." The only remaining question relates to the time when this completeness may be realized. Wesley says: "NOW, by faith, without doing or suffering more." Olshausen says: "In the concrete actuality, the complete idea, and, therefore, too, the crucifying of the old man, never appear completely realized." That is to say, the old man is completely crucified in the abstract, but in the concrete man he always lives! Common sense sides with the Englishman against the German.

Gal. 4:19: "My little children, of whom I travail in birth again until Christ be formed [aor.] in you." Here is a second spiritual birth, distinct from the first. All devout pastors find multitudes in their churches, rocking as old babes in the cradle of spiritual infancy, and they travail in birth for them, that the faint image of Christ enstamped upon them in their regeneration may be renewed and permanently deepened. Like coins on which the head of Liberty is but slightly impressed, they need to be placed beneath the die again, and receive a deep and clear impress. The aorist expresses the instantaneous reminting.

Eph. 1:13: "After that you believed [aor.] ye were sealed" [aor.]. Here the believing and the sealing are acts distinct, definite, and completed.

Eph. 2:5: "By grace ye have been saved" [perfect—and so continue].

Eph. 3:16-19: Here we have seven aorists in four verses—*grant, be strengthened, dwell,* or take up his abode, *may be able, to comprehend, to know,* and *be filled.* May we not infer that Paul chose this tense to convey most strongly and vividly the ability of Christ to do a great work in a short time, to save believers fully, and to endow them with the fullness of the Spirit? If gradual impartations of the Sanctifier had been in his thought, it is strange that he did not use one present tense to express endowment by degrees.

"The Greek perfect participles *rooted* and *grounded,*" says Dr. Karl Braune, "denote a state in which they already are and continue to be, which is the presupposition in order that they may be able to know."

The same writer, in Lange's *Commentary,* in his note on "to comprehend" [aor.], says that "it here means more than a mere intellectual apprehension, a perception, but pre-eminently an inward experience corresponding with 'to know' [aor.] in verse 19." "The aorist tense of 'to comprehend,'" says Ellicott, "perhaps implies the singleness of the act, and the middle voice—called by Krueger a dynamic middle—indicates the earnestness, or spiritual energy, with which the action is performed." How strongly does this grammatical examination of this passage confirm the essay of John Fletcher on the spiritual manifestation of Christ to the inward perception of the perfect believer by an instantaneous revelation!

Eph. 4:13: "Till we all attain [aor.] unto the unity of the faith and of the perfect knowledge of the Son of God, unto the full-grown man, unto the measure of the stature of the fullness of Christ."—*Alford's Version*

The perfecting of the saints is here expressed by a definite and momentary arrival at a point where faith merges into knowledge, where a Savior believed becomes a Savior fully realized. See Olshausen's full comment. This transition from faith to full knowledge is a crisis expressed by the aorist. It is when the Paraclete purges the film of inbred sin from the eye of the soul, and Jesus, as a living, loving, glorified, and complete Savior, is manifested to the spiritual vision. Then the child, the imperfect believer, becomes a perfect man, and reaches the fullness of Christ; that is, the abundance which he has to bestow, a fullness excluding all sin, but capable of eternal increase. That this point is before death is shown by the consequences which follow in the present life, as detailed in verses 14-16.

Eph. 5:25-26: "Husbands, be constantly loving [pres.] your wives, even as Christ loved [aor.] the Church." Says Ellicott: "The pure aoristic sense is more appropriate and more in accordance with the historic aorist that follows, so that 'gave' [aor.] is a specification of that wherein this love was pre-eminently shown. The moment is seized upon when his love culminated in the gift of his life for us." "That he might sanctify [aor.] and cleanse" [aor.]. Bishop Ellicott again says: "Both sanctification and purification are dependent on the atoning death of Christ. There is thus no necessity to modify the plain and natural meaning of the verb *to sanctify.* Here it neither implies simple consecration, on the one hand, nor expiation, absolution, on the other, but *the communication* and *infusion* of *holiness and moral purity.*" The tense indicates that it is a definite and momentary act.

Col. 1:9: "That ye might be filled [aor.] with the full knowledge of his will."

Phil. 3:12: "Not already perfected" (perfect), brought to the end of his course and crowned. The same word is used in the same sense in Luke 13:32. Paul and Jesus disclaim the same perfection. See Heb. 2:10; 5:9; 12:23.

Col. 3:5: "Mortify [aor., kill outright], therefore, your members which are upon the earth; fornication," etc. "Let nothing," says Bishop Ellicott, "live inimical to your true life, hidden in Christ. Kill at once [aor.] the organs and media of a merely earthly life." Here, in the very strongest terms, is the Wesleyan doctrine of entire sanctification as a distinct and instantaneous work of the Spirit clearly set forth. A young evangelist, holding meetings in a Baptist church, preached to pastor and people entire sanctification as immediately attainable by faith. The pastor was stumbled by the English reading of this text, "Mortify"; that is, keep mortifying day by day. He thought that he must ever keep a little sin alive in his heart in order to be forever mortifying it. His mistake was (1) in overlooking the real meaning of mortify, *to make dead,* and substituting the idea of repression; and (2) in disregarding the aorist tense of the command, enjoining a decisive and momentary act, to be done once for all.

Col. 3:8: "But now put off [aor.] all these: anger, wrath," etc. The aorist imperative is a broom that sweeps the heart clean at one stroke of omnipotent power.

Verse 12: "Put on [aor.], therefore," etc. By the incoming of the abiding Comforter all the excellences of the Christian character are to be at once assumed. This is the positive side of entire sanctification, the negative being the mortifying of sin in verse 5.

Verse 13: "Forbearing [pres.] and forgiving" [pres.]. There will be occasion for the constant exercise of these virtues.

Verse 15: "Let the peace of God rule [pres.] constantly, and be [pres.] ye thankful always."

Verse 16: "Let the word of God dwell [pres.] perpetually."

Verse 18: "Wives submit [pres.] yourselves constantly," etc.

Verse 19: "Husbands love [pres.] your wives at all times"—on washing days, when breakfast is late, and the bread is sour.

Verse 20: "Children obey [pres.] your parents constantly."

Verse 21: "Fathers provoke [pres.] not at any time your children."

Thus a series of present imperatives extends through this chapter and to verse 6 in chapter 4, enjoining daily recurring duties. But the aorist imperatives are always used when the duty of putting away sin from the heart, and putting on the fruits of the Spirit, is commanded. Let the candid reader examine this chapter, and he will see that the reason for the use of the aorists is that entire sanctification and the fullness of the Spirit are viewed as a work to be finished at a stroke, while duties to our fellow men are to be constantly repeated.

No other account can be given for the alternation of tenses in the imperatives in this chapter.

I Thess. 3:13: "To the end he may stablish [aor.] your hearts unblamable in holiness." Here the tense indicates a single and momentary act. The same Greek construction occurs in chapter 4:9 where the present tense is used, "to love one another," a constant duty. A similar form of expression in the Greek occurs in Hebrew 9:14: "to serve [pres.] the living God."

I Thess. 4:8: "Who also gave [aor.] unto us his Holy Spirit." Here the aorist is used, says Alford, "as being a great definite act of God by his Son." The act is just as definite whether the gift is dispensational or individual.

I Thess. 5:23: "And the very God of peace, once for all, sanctify [aor.] you wholly, and your whole spirit, and soul, and body he preserved" [initial aorist, to mark the beginning in the heart of the power that keeps the believer]. The nicety of Paul's grammatical knowledge is seen in verse 25: "Brethren, pray [pres.] for us. Greet [aor.] all the brethren with a holy kiss." The praying was to be continuous, the kissing momentary.

II Tim. 2:21: "Purge" [aor.]. *Sanctified* and *prepared* are both in the perfect tense, implying the permanent result of the definite act of purging.

Titus 2:14: The verbs *gave, redeem,* and *purify* are all aorists, indicating momentary acts. The purifying is before death, because its subjects are to be zealous of good works.

Titus 3:6: "Shed [aor.] on us abundantly": (1) To inaugurate a dispensation; (2) To sanctify and endow individuals.

Personal pentecosts have been experienced all along the ages. Paul received such a pentecost (Rom. 5:5).

Heb. 4:2: "Let us labor [hasten, aor.], therefore, to enter into that rest." A vigorous and earnest effort is enjoined. The word *labor* in Greek is radically the same as *haste* in Joshua 4:10. "And the people hasted [aor.] and passed over."

Heb. 13:12: "That he might sanctify [aor.] the people... suffered [aor.] without the gate."

I Pet. 1:15: "So become you [aor., by an all-surrendering act of faith] holy in all manner of conduct." Verse 16 (according to the received text): "Become ye [aor.] instantaneously holy, for I am holy." The aorist in these verses indicates a transition from sin to holiness, and not a progress.

I Pet. 3:15: "Sanctify [aor.] the Lord Christ in your hearts." Says Wiesinger, endorsed by Alford: "The addition of 'in your hearts' is added to the Old Testament quotation, to bring out that the sanctification must be perfected in the inner parts of a man, and so keep him from false fear." "Care only for this, that your heart may be a temple of Christ; then nothing will disturb you." This implies that there is a time when he becomes completely enthroned in the heart. Hence the precision of the aorist: Sanctify once for all a place for the Lord Christ, or Christ as Lord, in your hearts. See the critical reading of *Christ* for *God.* Verses 15-16 show the results in this life.

I Pet. 5:7: We copy Alford's note: "CASTING [aor., once for all, by an act which includes the life] ALL YOUR anxiety ['the whole of,' not every anxiety as it arises, for none will arise if this transference has been effectually made] UPON HIM.' The brackets are Alford's.

II Pet. 1:19: We have the highest authority for reading this without a parenthesis, which some put in, obscuring the sense. No passage of Scripture more strikingly describes the writer's Christian experience, first of painful doubt and then of cloudless assurance; first a spasmodic clinging of the intellect to the external evidences of miracle and prophecy, and then the sunrise—Christ manifested, the daystar in his heart. There are in this verse four verbs in the present tense, *have, do, take, shineth,* representing the alternation of light and darkness in early Christian experience. The lamp feebly glimmers in a gloomy, or, literally, *dirty* place, giving just light enough to see impurities, but not fire enough to consume them. In this twilight state doubts harass the soul, and there is an intense wishing and watching for the daydawn and the rising sun. To the patient waiter there is at last a tropical sunrise. The darkness flees, the filthy place is cleansed....

But how is this shown in the Greek text? Note the two aorist verbs *dawn* and *arise,* "putting an end," says Alford, "to the state indicated by the present participles above." What this daystar is Grotius, De Wette, and Huther best explain, who think that some state in the readers themselves is point ed at, which is to supervene upon a less perfect state. Says Huther: "The writer distinguishes between *two degrees* of Christian life; in the first, faith rests upon outward evidences; in the second, on inward revelations of the Spirit; in the first, each detail is believed separately as such; in the second, each is recognized as a necessary part of the whole. And hence, being in the former is naturally called a walking in a dismal, dirty place, in the light of a lamp or candle, while the being in the latter is a walking in the morning." Alford adds: "This latter I believe to be nearly the true account." Let us see what is taught here: (1) Two states of spiritual life, symbolized by lamplight and sunlight. (2) The aorist tense marks a sharply defined emergence from the first to the second, by the glorious King of day arising in the heart. This we believe to be a correct exegesis of this highly figurative and beautiful text. It accords with the experience of all who have entered into the definite experience of perfect love.

II Pet. 2:20: "After they escaped [aor.] the pollutions of the world through the full knowledge [*epignosis'*] of the Lord," etc. Verse 22: "The sow that was washed" [aor.].

Heb. 10:2: "Once purged [perfect], a cleansing once for all and permanent." Such have no more conscience, or consciousness, of sins.

Heb. 10:26: "For if we willfully sin [pres., enter upon a course of sin] after we receive [aor.] the full knowledge [*epignosis'*] of the truth," etc.

Heb. 13:20: "Make you perfect" [aor., an insulated act]. The workman and not the work is to be made perfect.

I John 1:9: "If we persistently confess [pres.] our sins, he is faithful and just to forgive [aor.] us our sins, and to cleanse [aor.] us from all unrighteousness. The cleansing is just as definite, distinct, and decisive as the forgiveness. Alford cannot escape the force of these aorists. "Observe the two verbs are aorists, because the purpose of the faithfulness and justice of God is to do each as one great complex act—to justify and to sanctify wholly and entirely." Düsterdieck says: "The death and blood of Christ are set forth in two aspects: (1) as a sin offering for our justification, and (2) as the purifying medium for our sanctification." If the purifying is to be by degrees, the present tense would have been used instead of the aorist. He pleads for gradual sanctification, but there is no more grammatical basis for it than there is for a progressive justification.

I John 2:1: "These things I write unto you, that ye sin [aor.] not even once. And if any man sin [aor., once, not habitually], we have [pres.] constantly an advocate," etc.

I John 2:27: Received [aor.] in an instant of time. The anointing of the high priest was an *act,* not a *process.*

I John 3:6: This text in the English favors the notion that the man who loves not his brother never knew God savingly. But the perfect of this verb "to know" has acquired a present meaning. (See Winer, page 290.) Says Alford: "*Have known,* and many other perfects, lose altogether their reference to the past event, and point simply to the present abiding effect of it." Hence Alford's version: "Whosoever sinneth seeth him not, neither knoweth him." He may have both seen (spiritually perceived) and known him, but he does not now.

I John 3:9: "Whosoever has been born [perfect, brought into permanent sonship] of God is not habitually sinning, for his seed is abiding in him and he is not able to be sinning because he has been born [perf.] of God." If the aorist tense had been used in this verse instead of the perfect, it would have been a strong proof text for the doctrine "Once in grace always in grace." But, says Alford: "The abiding force of this divine generation in a man excludes sin; where sin enters that force does not abide; the *has been born* [perf.] is in danger of becoming the *was born* [aor.]; a lost life instead of a living life. And so all such passages as this, instead of testifying, as Calvin would have this one do, to the doctrine of the final perseverance of the regenerate, do, in fact, bear witness to the opposite, namely, that, as the Church of England teaches, we need God's special grace every day to keep us in the state of salvation, from which every act and thought of sin puts us in peril of falling away."

The critical reader may find aorists in the Greek Testament which must imply a state and not an insulated act. These group themselves into the following classes.

1. Where no present tense is in use in the Greek.

2. Where the signification of the verb itself implies continuance, as to live, to abide, to walk, to keep, etc. Here the aorist marks the entrance upon the state, called an "inceptive aorist." (See *Hadley's Greek Grammar*, sec. 708.)

3. Unconnected and sudden aorist imperatives are used both in the New Testament and in classical authors to express the strong emotion of the speaker. (See II Tim. 4:2; Jas. 4:7-10.)

4. Rarely in the Greek Testament an habitual act is expressed by the aorist, when the period of its continuance is long past, and the course of action is viewed as a completed whole. See Alford on II Thessalonians 1:10 and I Peter 3:6.

The aorists of verbs denoting sanctification and perfection quoted in this essay belong to no one of these exceptional classes.

We have looked in vain to find one of these verbs in the imperfect tense when individuals are spoken of. The verb *hagiazo, to sanctify,* is always aorist or perfect. See Acts 20:32; 26:18; Rom. 15:16; I Cor. 1:2; II Tim. 2:21; Heb. 10:10, 29; Jude 1. The same may be said of the verbs *katharizo* and *hagnizo, to purify.* Our inference is that the energy of the Holy Spirit in the work of entire sanctification, however long the preparation, is put forth at a stroke by a momentary act. This is corroborated by the universal testimony of those who have experienced this grace.

INDEX TO BIBLE TEXTS